EVERY DAY'S A WEEKEND

BY

NEWTON HOCKEY

An Insider's Guide to Early Retirement and
Exotic Travel

National Library of Canada Cataloguing in Publication Data

Hockey, Newton, 1940-
  Every day's a weekend

Includes index.
  ISBN 1-55212-819-9

  1. Hockey, Newton, 1940- --Journeys. 2. Travel. I. Title.
G465.H62 2001   910.4   C2001-910953-9

TRAFFORD

This book was published *on-demand* **in cooperation with Trafford Publishing.**
On-demand publishing is a unique process and service of making a book available for retail sale to the public taking advantage of on-demand manufacturing and Internet marketing.
On-demand publishing includes promotions, retail sales, manufacturing, order fulfilment, accounting and collecting royalties on behalf of the author.

Suite 6E, 2333 Government St., Victoria, B.C. V8T 4P4, CANADA
Phone   250-383-6864   Toll-free   1-888-232-4444 (Canada & US)
Fax   250-383-6804   E-mail   sales@trafford.com
Web site   www.trafford.com   TRAFFORD PUBLISHING IS A DIVISION OF TRAFFORD HOLDINGS LTD.
Trafford Catalogue #01-0219   www.trafford.com/robots/01-0219.html

10   9   8   7   6   5   4   3   2

Acknowledgements

I was encouraged to write this book by my friend, Noulan Bowker, with whom I worked at one time as a business development manager. We had similar names and the same job title and were always being confused for each other by our colleagues. Noulan has contributed to a book on marketing called *Celebrate Marketing* so has been through the process of being published. He provided me with much welcome advice during the initial writing of my book.

Dr. Patricia Anderson was my editor who made numerous suggestions to make the book more readable. She corrected my grammar and deciphered my engineering jargon.

I must thank many other friends who have questioned my wife and me each time we have returned from a trip. Some of our friends seem to live vicariously through us, as they are unwilling to venture into the unknown. They think that some of the places we visit are too scary for them but I hope this book will alleviate their fears so that they may follow in our footsteps. I can assure them that they will safely enjoy themselves.

My wife, Noreen, is the one person who has made this book possible. When we first travelled together, before we were married, we knew that we could share the wonders of travel and enjoy life together. She has gone along with my wild travel ideas and come up with many of her own. We are a most compatible, complementary and mutually supportive couple. My role is the overall planning of our trips, and I also take lots of photographs and videos to record our experiences. Noreen keeps a detailed journal of our travels, which I found invaluable when I reviewed my first draft of the book. I had forgotten many places we had been and many incidents that had occurred. She has reviewed the book continuously during the writing and editing process and kept me on track. I am looking forward to many more years of travelling together and to writing more books.

Newton Hockey

West Vancouver
Canada

CONTENTS

EPILOGUE

APPENDIX :   Chronology

List of Maps

List of Photographs

Useful Resources

Noreen & Newton in Vancouver

Chapter 1

Dreams Become Reality

I have always dreamed of travelling the world. My Father died at age sixty-three after working hard all his life. He had travelled a little before he was married and had plans to travel again with my mother when my sister and I had finished our schooling. But he was cheated by cancer. I was determined to fulfil my travel ambitions while I was fit and young enough to do so.

My original plan was to ease into retirement by working three or four days a week as a high tech marketing consultant on Vancouver Island, British Columbia. House prices were cheaper there than in the city of Vancouver, and with the proceeds of my house in West Vancouver, I could have bought a nice little cottage in the country with a bit of land too. I could also have pursued my hobby of gardening, and travelled in my increased spare time. But all this changed when I met my wife, Noreen. She is a little younger than I am and wanted to continue part-time work as a nurse and live in the city. When we were married, we stayed on in West Vancouver and my revised plan was to carry on working as a consultant with easy hours.

My principal client ran into financial problems and stopped paying me, so I quit working. I quite liked my newfound leisure and soon realised that it would be better if my wife, Noreen, stopped working too so that we could spend more time together. There is a lot to do in a house and garden, and Vancouver is very fortunate to be near wonderful mountains on which to hike and ski. There was no shortage of things to keep us busy.

How can you afford to retire at fifty?

The answer to this question is different for everybody. What does your desired lifestyle cost? What can you give up? What assets do you have? Are you using them wisely?

We decided that we wanted to travel for up to six months a year but spend our summers in beautiful British Columbia. The first thing we did was to downsize our house and move into a townhouse, putting the money saved into investments. The second thing was to have someone share our townhouse with us to further reduce our costs. Another person would also be able to take care of the place while we were away. We tried this for two years and although it worked financially, the interpersonal relationships did not!

A better alternative was to rent out our home while we were away. This has worked for us on several occasions and given us extra cash for our travels. I realise that letting strangers use your home and effects is not for everyone, but we minimize worry and loss by locking up irreplaceable items and personal things, leaving out only what can be replaced. A damage deposit covers the cost of broken or missing items, and a video inventory of all your things is a useful way to make sure you don't overlook anything that might go missing.

We were fortunate not to have a mortgage on our home and realised that we could make productive use of its asset value. It is easy to borrow money against your house at the bank prime rate from banks or trust companies. It is also easy to invest the proceeds at a higher interest rate in mutual funds and to arrange for systematic withdrawals to pay the lender. That is what we did. The funds need to be watched carefully with the help of a professional to be certain of keeping ahead of the game. This is particularly important if one travels a lot.

An Unusual Investment

We became involved as a result of our travels in Costa Rica. A Vancouver based, limited partnership was developing a reforestation project in the north of the country. Natural jungles had been cut for ranch land and we were to replant teak trees to restore the forests.

The idea is to have a perpetually yielding forest of teak for commercial purposes. Teak is ideal because, once a tree is cut, the root system remains alive and sprouts a new tree. Trees are ready for cutting after only a dozen years, on average, so one doesn't have to wait too long to see a return on the investment and the potential return is quite significant. There are also income tax advantages from farm loss write-offs and deferring income until a more advantageous time when one's overall income is smaller. We have yet to receive any return on our investment, but the teak trees are growing well at the forecasted rate, while the world price of teak is still rising.

When you are retired, you have more time to shop wisely. You can find discounts and coupons for just about everything! Now, with the Internet, you can even print your own coupons from savingumoney.com. Travel deals on the World Wide Web allow you to get last minute trips at hugely discounted rates. One such site is www.flyaow.com, which has links to all the major airlines in the world. If you enjoy the thrill of an auction, try www.skyauction.com. And be sure to collect frequent flyer points on everything you purchase by using the right credit card, paying the balance in full every month to avoid interest. Other ways to save on travel include arranging group travel and joining travellers' organizations.

Free Travel

Group travel means lower costs for everyone involved. More importantly for the organizer, it can mean a free trip for every fifteen people in your group. It can also give you complimentary local transportation and meals. We called ourselves Trip Trimmers International and organized trips to Bali. Our computer-generated business cards worked wonders with the Indonesians, as they are impressed with the title of "tour leader". We subsequently changed our name from Trip Trimmers because some people actually thought they would lose weight on our trips. Now we are known as "Hot Tours."

The travellers' organization we joined is Servas, which was founded in the forties. It has host homes all over the world and was formed to promote peace and understanding between nations. You apply with references and, after an interview, you are supplied with a letter of introduction, which can be used to meet hosts for a two-night stay, totally free of charge. The benefit of this arrangement is immense. Each traveller has an immediate friend and contact almost anywhere and can quickly get into the life and culture of a totally foreign society. In return, the traveller brings news and information about his or her home country and discusses world issues. Naturally, a small gift from the home country is a welcome additional token of friendship. We have travelled extensively with Servas in the United States, Japan, Australia, New Zealand, Africa and the United Kingdom. Other travellers' organizations offer similar benefits.

Home Exchange

House swapping is gaining popularity and there are several agencies that can put you in touch with house owners in many parts of the world. The big advantage to house swapping is that you have all you need in someone else's home, including a car, and you are comforted by the fact that you will each be treating the other's belongings with respect. We have heard of lots of good experiences from those who have tried it.

We only did it once, with an old high school friend of mine in England, and it worked very well. We overlapped with each other at either end of the three-week exchange so that we could have some time together.

The disadvantage of swapping houses is that you can be stuck in the same place for longer than you would wish. When we travel, we tend to want to move on to different parts of the country after a few days. We would only make an exception when we find a wonderful tropical beach town. Houses to exchange are hard to find in these areas, although, we have managed to housesit for expatriates in Honduras while they made short trips out of the country.

We have even had to turn down the chance to house-sit for six months in a beautiful home with a pool in a Caribbean beach town, because it coincided with summer in Vancouver. All our travelling takes place in the winter months so that we miss the wettest weather of the west coast of Canada. We can only be out of the country for six months a year in order to maintain our medical insurance coverage at home and while travelling.

A word about time-share projects. We were actually tempted to invest in a time-share condominium development that came with a lifetime offer of wonderful exotic vacations in any part of the world. At that time, the investment would have been about $10,000 and annual maintenance fees about $100. The system imposed numerous conditions, which made your first choice of time and location almost impossible to achieve. It does work for some people who wish to go to a fancy resort and pamper themselves for a week or two every year. It certainly would not work for us, as we like to travel for much longer periods and for much less money. Even so, it is not a bad idea to attend time-share presentations just for the goodies they offer. We have received numerous dinners out, car rental in Bali; accommodation in Whistler Ski Resort and Penticton, British Columbia; ferry tickets to Cozumel, Mexico; and a Radio-Cassette Player. My wife vows never to attend another boring presentation again, but sometimes the offers are too good to turn down!

At Home in Vancouver

We spend our time at home in Vancouver on many activities, including the going-away and welcome-home parties. We also do considerable research and planning for upcoming trips and generally have an outline plan covering up to three years. We arrange for automatic payment of our finances, utility bills, insurance premiums, professional association memberships, et cetera, but we still have to check all these things before we leave on an extended trip. It is also a good idea to have a trusted friend, with a power of attorney, to take care of unexpected events and expenses.

"The Rainbow Maker" TM

Various projects have presented themselves to us, most notably "The Rainbow Maker". This a novelty item that you hang in a sunny window, and which produces beautiful rainbow coloured stripes on walls, ceilings and even people. It is made of a plastic material with very fine prisms on one side. On the other side is a silk-screened design, which may be a dolphin, killer whale, unicorn or a dozen other designs. Two friends, who subsequently became my partners in the business, introduced me to the product after the first-generation version had been designed and sold at local art and gift shows in Vancouver. I immediately saw the potential-- after all, everyone loves a rainbow. We refined the product and began to manufacture it in our basements and on our dining room tables.

Our first efforts at marketing involved visiting stores in the lower mainland of British Columbia; my wife and I also sold from the trunk of our car. The best stores for us were science and nature stores, hospital gift shops, the Vancouver Aquarium, Science World and New Age shops. Next we took a booth in the California Gift Show in San Francisco, made a big splash of colour, sold to a score of gift shops, and signed up an agent who covered four states.

The next problem was how to fill the orders. I was the only retired partner, so it was left to Noreen and me to process the orders. We had to assemble the product, which had been silk-screened by one of my partners, and box and ship it to customers all over the west coast of the U.S.A. and Canada. We were overwhelmed and sought help from neighbourhood children who would come to our garage after school and at weekends to work in the sweatshop we came to call "The Factory." In this way we could clear the dining room of plastic, frames, packaging and boxes, and even have time to ourselves.

This frantic activity went on all one summer, and when the children went back to school, our inventory started to go down fast. The whole project was severely impacting on our retirement status, and this would never do!

The distributor of "The Rainbow Maker" in Eastern Canada was interested in making the product, so we signed a contract with him to manufacture it in Ontario in return for a modest royalty. We would also ship him the raw material and provide him with new designs from time to time. The first new design was a Star on a suction cup, which could be applied to a window. This was an instant success and has subsequently surpassed the sales of all previous designs.

This retirement project, which almost got out of control, kept us busy for eleven months and made money from day one. Not much money, true, but enough for a lot of dinners out--which is how we judged our success. In the nine years we have been collecting royalties, we have enjoyed many more dinners out. We are now thinking of restarting our marketing efforts using the Internet and are still figuring out how to get other people to do the work while we continue to play.

The Wobbley Wheelers

Cycling has become a frequent activity with us since we retired. My first bike was an old ten speed that had belonged to my son. It was quite a smart looking silver bike but the gears were never low enough for me. Whichever direction I took when leaving my home, I had to climb small hills.

We used to go to an illegal pub every two weeks in a friend's house in North Vancouver, and on the notice board there we saw a newsletter from a cycling club whose name attracted us. It was the "Wobbley Wheelers" and it was started and run by Michael Hart who happened to be in the pub that night. We were introduced to Michael and I immediately liked his British sense of humour. In no time at all we had become rude to each other, a good sign if you are British. North Americans sometimes have difficulty in handling this rudeness between two Brits; in fact, Michael's girlfriends have expressed concern to him about this on several occasions. Noreen has become used to and amused by it. Anyway, at our first meeting, Michael convinced us that we should go out with the "Wobbley Wheelers" the following Sunday.

Now the criteria for a Wobbley ride are that it be flat, not too long, and finish at a suitable watering hole for brunch. In addition, if the weather was poor, we would still meet but miss the ride and go straight to brunch. True to its billing in the Wobbley newsletter, the ride was flat, so flat that even I enjoyed it until I fell off my bike. About a dozen or so riders were drifting along a deserted road beside a river and I, being social, was riding three abreast between two women at the rear. One of them, a regular Wobbley rider, wobbled, forcing me to take evasive action. I swerved out of control; my bike crashed to the ground and my head hit the pavement, right in the path of the only truck within five miles of us. Someone must have been trying to give me a strong message as fortunately the truck also swerved and missed my head by a foot (if you get what I mean).

I was lucky and received only minor scrapes and bruises. It was my first Wobbley ride, and I made the front and only page of the "Wobbley Wheelers" newsletter the following week. The lessons I learned were that my cycling helmet was a good investment, that one should not ride more than two abreast and that I needed more practice riding my bike.

We started riding every week, when the weather was good of course, and slowly started to develop muscles that we had never seen before. The saddle sores persisted until we found a gel seat, which spread the load and cushioned the bumps. As a new member of the club you are permitted one ride before you are required to purchase a Wobbley tee shirt. When we were selecting a colour for the shirts, Michael and I couldn't agree; he wanted an insipid yellow and I favoured a fashionable teal. We finally settled on a bright red for danger. The purchase of a Wobbley shirt entitles you to lifetime membership in the club and there are now about a hundred and fifty life members. Each shirt is customized to the individual by naming his or her hometown on the back. Several countries are represented and shirts have found their way to many parts of the globe.

Cycling became an enjoyable pastime and we would head out during the week, not just on Sundays. After all, every day was a weekend for us. We were now experienced riders and felt quite superior when new members joined our club. Sometimes they would turn up with old ladies' bike, complete with basket in front but no gears. They would find the ride hard but enjoy the company. At the next garage sale they would pick up a slightly better bike and slowly become more proficient cyclists.

Some went on to outfit themselves with tight fitting cyclist's garb and really fancy bicycles, and would even leave the club, as it wasn't fast enough for them. Not our fearless leader, though. Michael was a real cyclist dedicated to spreading the word about the benefits of cycling as a sport and for exercise. He would ride from the front of the pack to the back and back again, constantly rounding up his flock of cyclists like an anxious sheepdog. He was very fit and kept that way by cycling fifty miles before breakfast most mornings.

Members of the "Wobbley Wheelers" come from all walks (or should that be cycles?) of life, and from all ages and marital states. It is an excellent social club and you get effortless exercise thrown in. Over the years, we have developed lasting friendships, which I value highly. We have been on holiday with a number of members, although we do not usually use the terms "holiday" or "vacation" ourselves, as we prefer the term "life".

A favourite trip we have taken a couple of times follows the Kettle Valley line, a disused railway route in the interior of British Columbia. We usually go for four days and arrange to stay in small hotels or rustic resorts on the way. Riding over railway grades is easy and takes you through beautiful countryside well away from roads. You see some old mining ghost towns and lots of wildlife such as bear, elk, deer, wolverine, fox and eagles, to name a few. We have people who come from England and San Francisco to ride with us every year.

There is one ride we shall probably not repeat. This is on one of the Gulf Islands between Vancouver and Vancouver Island. Saltspring Island's hills are formidable and were not popular with the less experienced amongst us. I hasten to say that Noreen and I had no problems coping with hills, as we keep in shape by cycling up some reasonable mountains around Vancouver.

Hiking

We also keep in shape is by hiking the mountains near our home in West Vancouver and sometimes further afield, too. We like to hike in the middle of the week to avoid the crowds on the local trails. This can be a little hazardous as we frequently see bears when the trails are quiet.

One way of overcoming this problem is to have a dog with us. We do not have one of our own, as this would make it impossible to travel for six months a year. But we had the next best thing--or it may actually be the best idea of all--we had access to a beautiful Golden Retriever, called Sake, who was left on her own all day while her owners were at work. We rescued Sake and took her with us on our hikes. She thought this was great, of course, and her owners appreciated it too. It was truly a win, win, win situation. It was a sad day when we were in Africa and heard by e-mail that Sake had to be put down. She has fortunately been replaced with another Golden called Mocha, and we look forward to many years of walks with our "rent-a-dog."

We love dogs--well at least the big, obedient ones--and we would like one of our own, but that will have to wait until we are too old to travel. Then, perhaps, we shall settle down to life in a little cottage in the country somewhere. The property will have to include a garden for the dog to run in and a greenhouse for me to play in. Maybe we shall even breed Golden Retrievers. Sometimes we are asked to dog-sit for friends and we enjoy this, as it gives us a change in routine and often a nice house along with it. We don't accept payment for this but there are perks such as swimming pools and tennis courts.

"Movie Stars"

For two summers in Vancouver, we took up a part-time career as movie extras though rather prefer the term "background actors." We found a new talent agent who was advertising in the local newspaper for new faces and signed up with her. At first we worked two or three times a week and were paid the minimum wage. We enjoyed learning about the business and meeting the other extras and some of the actors, directors and crew.

We now know something about what goes on in those fancy trailers and changing rooms you see when a movie is being filmed on location. Often the food is very good and there are always snacks and drinks available. Some people think we must get bored, hanging around all day for a few minutes of action. I never even took a book to the set, as there was always something to see or people to talk with. We would often be asked to dress formally for dinner or dance scenes and that was quite fun too. We worked alongside actors such as Anthony Quinn, Brad Pitt, John Travolta and Kirstie Alley. I was a stand-in for Judd Hirsch once. Some of the films were feature films like *Legends of the Fall;* others were television movies of the week, and we also worked on several series such as *X-Files* and *The Commish*. Noreen was chosen to be a nurse on many occasions, while I was a doctor and lawyer on some sets. As we became more proficient and known by casting directors, we got more work and better pay. We could have made a full time job of it, had we wished. But it started to interfere with our retirement, so we stopped before we reached our peak. Who knows, if we had continued to work, we might have been "discovered."

We love Vancouver and enjoy showing it off to visitors. We joined a club called Vancouver AM which is a tourist services organization. Its members are mostly involved in the tourist business, and they meet every Friday at 7:30 A.M. to network and listen to topical speakers. They are a very high-energy group, and we quickly became involved with the running of it.

It was there that we met Dee Nelson, a newcomer to town. She claimed to be the daughter of Howard Hughes, the super-wealthy industrialist who left an enormous estate. Somehow we became involved in an international news conference where Dee announced her claim to the family fortune. She also announced her name to be Dee Sharp Hughes Nelson. Unfortunately, she was paranoid about being followed by FBI agents and others who were setting fires in her apartment building. She alleged that they were conspiring to discredit her and stop her from inheriting millions of dollars from her late father's estate. On top of this, her alleged mother, Mrs. Sharp, distanced herself from Dee on national television. We did enjoy meeting Dee, as she was a colourful character. She was particularly great, dressed as a clown, entertaining children. At Christmastime, we took her "lobbying," our term for visiting the beautifully decorated hotel lobbies in Vancouver. Eventually she returned to California and disappeared from our lives.

Retirement is a happy and busy time for us. During the first ten years, we have accomplished a lot but there is so much more to do and so many places left to visit. We treat every day as a weekend and life as one long vacation packed with enjoyable activities. It helps that my wife and I enjoy doing the same things and can stand each other's company almost constantly. It would have been nicer to retire at *forty,* instead of fifty.

Laos

* Chang Rai

* Chang Mai

Isan

* Phitsanulok

* Khon Kaen

Khorat
*

Bangkok
*

Cambodia

Ko Chang

Ko Samui

Phuket

THAILAND

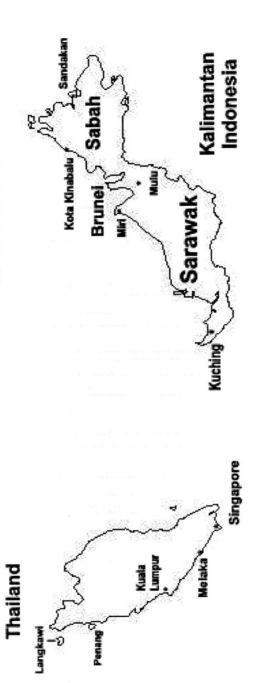

Borneo

Sabah

Sandakan

Kalimantan
Indonesia

Kota Kinabalu

Brunei

Mulu

Miri

Sarawak

Kuching

Thailand

Langkawi

Penang

Kuala
Lumpur

Melaka

Singapore

MALAYSIA

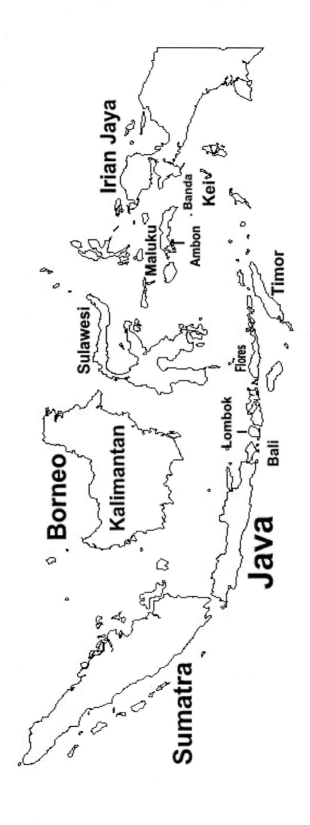

INDONESIA

Chapter 2

Oriental Odyssey

Spanish is not required in Asia. We had taken an introductory course in Spanish at night school in readiness for a proposed trip to South America. Our travel plans were shaken after three groups of younger travellers visited us during the summer after their tours of south-east Asia. They were so enthusiastic about the area, especially Bali, Indonesia, that we decided to change our destination to Asia. We had to study hard for two months using the library, our friends and our bible, *The Lonely Planet Guide to South-East Asia.*

We set out in October with our brand new convertible backpacks. We were not sure that we were still young enough to be sleeping in hostels and were concerned that the budget places listed in *The Lonely Planet* would not be comfortable enough for our mature bodies and refined tastes. The backpacks could be converted into reasonably presentable soft-sided suitcases and the Hyatt would always accept us. At first the packs seemed so heavy and we could hardly walk. Was this really going to be fun?

Hong Kong

Frequent flyer points, gathered during my working years, gave us two tickets to Bangkok via Hong Kong, so we stopped first in Hong Kong expecting that a week in the city would be more than enough. We checked into the YWCA, which was clean and comfortable and well within our budget.

The first day we got our bearings by walking and bussing around Mongkok, the central business district on the mainland peninsular of Hong Kong. Immediately we were all too aware that we were foreigners and felt very conspicuous. We checked out the Star Ferry and the frantic waterfront and spent a peaceful hour in Kowloon Park. We visited up-scale shops and local markets including the night market.

On the second morning, we telephoned Joanne, the sister of a friend we knew in Vancouver, to say hello and to see if we could meet her and her husband for dinner. Joanne worked in the Canadian Consulate and we found her at work. When she heard we were staying at the Y, she immediately said that we should pack up and come to stay at their apartment on Hong Kong Island. She would not listen to our protests that we were happy at the Y, and the next thing, we were on the subway at the tail end of the morning rush hour. We were packed in like sardines; never before had we seen so many people in such a small space. At the Consulate, we picked up the key to Joanne's apartment and made our way by taxi to a luxurious suite with fabulous views over the island, and across to Kowloon on the mainland.

It is so nice to know people in a strange city. They shorten the learning curve for you and recommend sights to see and things to do that are not in the guidebooks. We did the usual trips to Aberdeen Market, the floating restaurants, Stanley and the New Territories, and bussed all over the island and Kowloon. We also discovered that Hong Kong is so much more than that. We found our way by various ferries to some of the other islands and even found ourselves alone on a deserted hillside near a Trappist monastery.

We had thought that Hong Kong was an overcrowded city with every square inch occupied by something or someone. Another thing that impressed us was the number and variety of watercraft carrying people and cargo in all directions. There were junks, hovercraft, catamarans, tugs and barges of all sizes, sailboats, power boats, steam boats and row boats to name a few; all were tearing around at top speed creating enormous wakes which threatened to capsize the more fragile craft. We were also tearing around trying to see everything and do everything.

China

China and Macau were so close that we had to see them too. Tour companies arranged all the details of visas, transport and accommodations, making it simple to do a three or four day round trip to get a feel for the industrial south of China. We joined a group that included a Dutch girl called Leona who worked in Munich for British Airways, four New Yorkers, Randy from Haiti, two Aussies and two Swedes. One guide took us to Macau, another escorted us through the border to China, and a third took over the China tour.

The memory I have of China, albeit limited to a tiny area, is of a very crowded, squalid, industrial area with thousands of tiny apartments in large groups of high rise buildings. And I can still picture the hundreds of cyclists, the dirty streets and littered streams. We stopped at the birthplace and museum of Dr. Sun Yat Sen and peered into a school classroom packed with students learning algebra. The children were pleased to see and talk to us.

On our first night in China, we stayed in an approved hotel in a small town. We immediately walked into the centre through scores of cyclists to explore and meet some people. Leona caused quite a stir, as she was tall for a woman and a giant compared to the Chinese. When she had a shoeshine on the street, she became a little confused over the Chinese currency and became involved in a small argument. Soon she was completely surrounded by a huge crowd and we had to wade into the crowd to rescue her.

The next day, we were supposed to see pottery and ceramic factories but they were closed--so much for an organized tour! We did see a temple and an antiquated silk factory. In the restaurants, the waitresses were most rude. We were not liking our China trip very much.

In Canton, we saw puppies in the window of a restaurant and immediately hurried back to our comfortable westernized hotel. We were glad to take the catamaran back to over-civilized Hong Kong. We had been over-exposed to unfamiliar sights, common in undeveloped countries, and this was our first Asian encounter. Our first ten days were over and we were starting to go into sensory overload.

Bangkok, Thailand

Bangkok was our next stop and we arrived at nine o'clock in the evening. This was late but we had made a reservation in a hotel recommended to us by friends at home. We knew that a train could take us to the city from the airport and we could complete our journey by an approved taxi. We made our way to the train station at the airport, passing a group of taxi drivers who told us that the last train of the evening had left. Naturally we didn't believe them, as it was only 9:00 P.M. After we struggled all the way to the platform with our heavy packs, we found that indeed the last train had left and that the only way to the city was by taxi.

We humbly returned to the waiting "taxis" and stuffed our bags into the trunk of the first, not checking, as we had been told, to verify that it was indeed a legal taxi. Only when we were on our way did we realize that this was a pirate taxi. It was taking us at high speeds in an undetermined direction through streets with indecipherable names in a totally foreign script. We were nervous. Where were we being taken? The driver stopped to ask directions and showed someone the card for our hotel. The next thing we knew, we were outside our hotel and our luggage was being whisked inside. Panic over!

When we awoke the next morning, we thought that we were in Venice. Torrential rains during the night had turned the streets into canals. After breakfast, the floods began to subside and we were able to take a taxi to explore the city.

Bangkok is a bustling, vibrant, noisy city consumed with diesel and petrol fumes. Many of the locals and police wear protective masks over their faces. It is full of honking tuk-tuks; the local motorcycle engine driven tricycles that need no horns as they make so much noise anyway. We had to try one, of course, and an exciting drive it was. We were whisked through the frantic traffic at breakneck speed punctuated by full stops in gridlocked jams. This was in 1992, before the new elevated freeways were officially open. I understand from friends now that even with the freeways open, traffic is still a nightmare.

We had another friend of a friend to contact in Bangkok, and it turned out that he was a project manager for the freeway construction. He told us of hours spent in his car going just a few miles through the city. He would take his in-tray with him from the office and deal with his correspondence in the comfort of his air-conditioned, chauffeur driven car.

When we arranged to meet him for dinner one night, he sent his car to pick us up. It was amazing how quickly we travelled the ten miles to his house. The driver was authorized to use the yet unopened freeway, and we were in the only vehicle on an empty highway. As we drove, we overlooked the seething mass of polluting cars, tuk-tuks, trucks and buses below. The restaurant where we dined was huge. It featured an enormous menu, which we couldn't understand, and the plates emerging from the kitchens were loaded with wonderful, colourful vegetables, meats and fish. The smells were tantalizing and the chillies hot, hot, hot. There was entertainment with dancing, singing and bands and the energy level was electric.

Back on the streets the cooking continued. On every corner, in every alleyway there were stalls cooking up a storm in woks or on grills. The smoke of charcoal mingled with the smell of the food stimulated the gastric juices once again and we were tempted, but resisted, the urge to taste. Our western stomachs would be pushed to resist the eastern bacteria lurking in the meats which had been hanging with flies all day.

Noreen, being a nurse, was fully aware of the consequences of getting sick in a foreign country. She had dealt with many a returning student in the health service of Simon Fraser University. She kept me from trying those succulent stir-fries and skewers of mystery meats covered with syrupy peanut sauce. Delicious fruits of all shapes and colours, ready to eat, were proffered. All fruit had to be peeled by us, said the guidebook, and all salads washed with purified water. The outdoor food stalls had to be avoided.

Sightseeing in Bangkok bewilders you with its scope and variety. The over-opulent Royal Palace contrasted with the poor in their shanties. The land markets bustling with crowds on foot were quite different from the floating markets on the river tributaries, where boats jostled for position to view and buy the multicoloured produce. We chartered our own speedboat for a couple of hours to explore the myriad of canals alongside the giant river that divides the city. Temples abound and we visited a few, learning that the dress code is strictly enforced. Noreen was prevented from entering one temple because she had no strap at the back of her sandals. We had to buy suitable shoes from a merchant a few yards away, who happened to have the right kind shoe in all sizes. I had no problem in spite of being very casually dressed--I was a man after all and the rules were different!

You can get a good feel for the city in a few days, and our plan was to see as much of Thailand as we could in three weeks. We headed for the railway station to buy our tickets to Chang Mai in the north. The station was very confusing to us, as we could not read the signs and no-one spoke English. A million people were rushing in all directions and the P.A. system was blaring announcements in panic mode. We thought that we would never find the right ticket office, let alone make the clerk understand what we wanted. In the end, we did. We booked an overnight train with sleeping accommodation for the following night and returned to the safety and comfort of our hotel to go over our proposed plans to tour the Golden Triangle of Thailand, Laos and Burma - now called Myanmar.

Northern Thailand

The train journey was comfortable, but we were entertained by the odd giant cockroach that also wanted to visit the north. The other passengers were very friendly and offered to share their food with us. There were also plenty of vendors plying the corridors with all kinds of food and drinks. There was constant entertainment around us, and in the daylight hours, the views through the windows were of steamy jungles and open rice fields. Horses, oxen, buffaloes, men and women worked the fields of green, green rice, peanuts and other crops.

The journey was long but enjoyable. In Chiang Mai, our hotel was geared to travellers, and we had many options for exploring the area and visiting the neighbouring Hill Tribes. It was near the end of the rainy season and it was still raining; I had a cold, so we decided to postpone the idea of trekking. We hoped it would dry up by the time we reached Chiang Rai.

The Chiang Mai hotel was called Sarah's Guest House and Sarah's husband, Jack, took us to see pottery, jade and umbrella factories. Jack had been a monk for three years and he was the perfect guide to take us to a temple ceremony. We were the only foreigners in the temple, and the worshippers welcomed us warmly. They involved us in their ceremony by placing our hands on a chain that everyone held while the priests performed their rituals. Many people had brought offerings for the monks who rely on donations for their living; we left some money, which was appreciated. We felt privileged to be included.

We headed further north by bus from Chiang Mai to Chiang Rai and then drove by van with other travellers to the Golden Triangle. This is the centre of the drug producing and trafficking area, situated on the Mekong River at the borders of Thailand, Laos and Burma. Apart from the scenery of green rice-fields and the murky Mekong River, there was nothing spectacular to report, but we did look suspiciously at everyone, thinking they must be involved in drug deals.

Further back at the land border with Burma, we had tried to cross the bridge to Burma but were prevented, not by the Burmese but by Thai officials. We did manage to meet some Burmese who had crossed into Thailand and had the chance to pick up some souvenirs and take photographs of children in their beautiful coloured costumes. I had one child hold my hand for ages just for the contact, while we strolled along. She did not expect a handout, but I gave her some candies. We linked up with a couple from Taiwan and hired a van to drive to the villages, since the rains would make our original plan of trekking most uncomfortable.

The tribes visited by us had migrated from Tibet and Burma centuries ago and sported their traditional dress, including intricately beaded headdresses. They were extremely poor and lived in deplorable conditions. They worked in their fields, scraping a living somehow, and a few sold souvenirs to the handful of impoverished travellers passing through. Noreen bought a head-dress, which is now a great conversation piece on our hall stand at home. The scenery was spectacular with mountains rising all around us and steep, green valleys below. Northern Thailand was interesting enough but we wanted to press on to the North-East and to the less travelled area known as Isaan.

North-East Thailand

We travelled by train from Chiang Mai to Phitsanulok, where we found a smart local restaurant with a small musical group and singer singing Thai songs. We were shown to the best table in the house and settled to read the menu and listen to the local music. This didn't happen, though; the musicians changed to Western music to make us feel at home! Fortunately, they didn't change the food. We enjoy hot and spicy food but were not prepared for the steaming pot of green Thai chicken curry brought to our table--it was the hottest food we had ever tasted in our lives. Nothing has beaten it since, either, but it was delicious and we did our best to eat it, liberally washing it down with Singha beer.

Markets are always an attraction for us, as they give us a feel for how the ordinary people live. The huge piles of red and green chillies in the markets of Isaan really made an impression on us. There would be not one but a dozen such piles in sight, each over a metre high. The heat would be enough to fire a power station! Besides the wonderful produce on display, there were the usual cooking stations with fabulous smells emanating and mixing together to make your gastric juices flow like water. Noreen again reminded me that we should not be tempted but we were and resisted. In retrospect, we would probably have been all right if we had stuck to foods other than meats that had been deep-fried or grilled in front of us.

The first part of our journey was easy. In Bangkok, we had bought rail passes that were valid for all our time in the country. The problem was that the railways don't go everywhere and our trip east from Chiang Mai didn't take us far. Consequently we had to change our mode of transport to the local bus.

Before we did that, though, we thought we would be smart and try to book our tickets from Bangkok, south to the Malaysian border. This was easier said than done, and I spent a lot of time going between offices at the train station in Phitsanulok and, in the end, was not at all certain what I had achieved. It seemed that the only place where I could be sure of our reservation was in Bangkok. The trains are all booked up days in advance and we didn't have days to spare. There was no way we wanted to be stuck in dirty old Bangkok waiting days for a train out.

We left the station to try out the buses. Some were comfortable and partly air-conditioned; others had wooden bench seats and open windows. We were the only foreigners around and were quite a curiosity. Through smiles and gestures, the Thais communicated to us that they were pleased to see us, and they made us feel welcome. At the frequent stops, girls selling everything from fully cooked meals to fruit and ice cream would board the bus. The roads wandered through jungles and mountains with spectacular scenery. When we stopped to change buses, there was always someone to help us. The same was true when we wanted to find a hotel for the night--a helpful man went out of his way to guide us through the streets and help us check in.

Normally we stayed in pretty modest accommodations but in Nakhon Ratchasima, also known as Khorat, we decided to splurge on a good hotel, which was very inexpensive by North American standards. The hotel was being expanded and they were adding several floors to the existing structure. We were quite happy there and removed the courtesy soaps, shampoo and matches to take home as souvenirs. I don't know how we found room in our back packs but somehow we did and, anyway, the packs seemed to be getting lighter as we became stronger. Later, when we had returned home, we learned that some floors of a hotel in Thailand had collapsed, killing a number of residents. We checked our souvenir shampoos and matches and found that it was the hotel in which we had stayed.

Ko Chang, South-East Thailand

We continued our journey by bus to Chanthaburi and then east to Trat and Laem Ngop, where we were to take a ferry to the island of Ko Chang, which is close to the Cambodian border. We enquired at the ticket office on the dock about how to go over to see our friend, David from North Vancouver, who was running a resort with his Thai girlfriend. We were told that a ferry would be leaving in a couple of hours and the office kindly offered to look after our packs while we had lunch at a restaurant at the end of the dock. We ordered lunch and were enjoying a drink while watching the activities of people and boats, when a man ran up to us and told us to follow him at once. We apologized to the waiter and hurried to the office to pick up our packs, but they were not there. We felt slight panic but continued to follow our guide another hundred yards down the dock. There, he pointed out an overloaded fishing boat with scores of people, sacks of rice and lumps of ice. He kept saying "Ko Chang, Ko Chang, David, David," and there on the top of a pile of vegetables were our packs. The boat was just casting off as we jumped aboard. Panic over.

The trip to the island was smooth and we enjoyed the interaction with the locals. We noticed a Vancouver Canucks hockey team cap on one young man--David had obviously been this way before. The dock where the boat landed was a mere foot wide and it was difficult enough to walk along with our packs, but all the freight was also carried on the narrow wiggley planks on the backs of strong men. We had to wait a while until all the people and cargo was discharged and then it began to rain, really rain. It was the end of the monsoon season after all.

Small trucks and jeeps were loaded until they groaned and then the first one set off up the muddy hill from the dock. Our turn came next and Noreen and I were told to stand on the rear bumper of our truck and hang on to the roof while the truck made a run for the hill. We did all right and passed the first truck, which was stuck in the mud near the top. Then we had to pull the first truck out of the mud in the torrential rain. We were completely soaked through but it was warm water and we laughed a lot. (Noreen commented that she felt as though we were in the movie *Raiders of the Lost Arc).*

Further on the trip across the island, we were invited into the cab of the truck and managed to take some videos of our trek up unbelievably rough hills, through rivers and, finally, to the beach on the other side. "Welcome to Sun Sai Resort," it said in front of a bunch of bamboo huts on the beach. We had arrived at David's place.

A sign announcing a monsoon special on room rates greeted us. This gave us mixed feelings as the pleasure of an inexpensive room was mitigated by our thoughts of rain on the beach. We need not have been concerned as the weather was fine and the little rain we had each day did not impede our enjoyment of warm temperatures, sunny skies, a blue sea and sandy beaches. We snorkelled in the clear waters, trekked through jungles to waterfalls and also explored the island by motorbike. Our planned few days stay turned into ten days of total relaxation in a wonderful, if rustic, seaside resort.

There was no electricity when we were there but hurricane lamps and candles enhanced the evening atmosphere. The food was superb and the beer cold and quenching. The atmosphere was laid-back to say the least and we kept our own record of drinks taken from the bar. By this time, Noreen let her guard down a bit on the matter of food and we were able to enjoy gourmet meals and salads. All the food was carefully washed in purified water and cooked well under the careful supervision of David and his girlfriend, Eck.

The travellers who passed through were all interesting people and shared their experiences with us, so that based on their latest intelligence reports, we were able to refine our itinerary through the rest of Thailand, Malaysia and Indonesia. Now, seven years later, we are still in touch with some of the people we met in Sun Sai. First it was through the exchange of postcards from various places around the world and now it is via e-mail. The island of Ko Chang has changed, we have heard. More tourists have found this tropical paradise and now there is even electricity on the island.

Our trip resumed with the bus ride to Bangkok where we stayed one night at our safe hotel, Borarn House, before tackling the railway station again. It was much easier this time and far less confusing and overwhelming. We had learned a lot in our travels already and were able to cope with the seeming bedlam, so much so, that the reservations we had made from North-East Thailand were found and we secured our sleeping car for the long rail ride down peninsular Thailand to Malaysia.

Malaysia

Malaysia welcomed us with signs threatening the mandatory death sentence if we were found carrying drugs. We were carrying syringes, but no drugs, and we had a note from our doctor stating that the syringes were for emergency use by a doctor in case no clean ones were available. Customs searched our bags for new books, which were subject to heavy duties. All our books were well used, as they had been read by many travellers and exchanged several times over the past six weeks. We left the station at the border and found a taxi to take us to the ferry for the island called Langkawi. It is a resort island being developed for tourism by the government of Malaysia, and we noticed new hotels and a golf course under construction.

Our guidebook listed some budget accommodations and we found one next to a new hotel on a lovely beach. We paid about ten dollars a day and the people next door paid over ten times that. We met some of the rich people on the beach one day and they invited us back to their hotel for a drink at their pool. The hotel staff was most courteous and brought us towels and drinks. We went again the following day and received the same treatment.

This time, though, we did not have our hosts with us, as they had checked out. But it didn't matter in the least to the staff.

The washrooms in the hotel were western style, which was a novelty to us--we had been used to the eastern hole-in-the-ground variety. We were curious about scuff marks on the toilet seats until we realized that some of the local Malaysians were not used to sitting and preferred to squat on the seat. Later we noticed signs indicating how one should use a western toilet.

Another custom, which intrigued us, was the women's practice of swimming in their street clothes. Moslem women keep themselves well covered at all times, exposing only their hands, feet and faces. This also applies when they swim, and they simply walk into the water, dressed as they are. The warm sun dries their clothes in a short while. A group of Moslem factory girls on a company paid weekend outing moved into the hut next to ours. There were about ten of them in a hut designed for two. They swam in their long sleeved tee shirts and trousers but when it came time to leave for home, they changed into the most beautifully coloured saris. We took photographs and exchanged addresses so we could send them prints.

After a few more days exploring trails, waterfalls and beaches around the island we took another ferry, this time to Penang. Georgetown is the principal town on the island and we explored it briefly on foot and in tri-shaws. We noticed the wide ethnic diversity of the population and this was reflected in the restaurants, which offered all kinds of foods. We elected for Indian on our only night there, and it was superb. We knew we were passing that way again on our return home through Malaysia and

Thailand, so we pushed on to Sumatra, Indonesia, the next morning.

Sumatra, Indonesia

The ferry ride was uneventful and we saw no other foreign tourists on the crowded boat. Medan, a highly industrialized city, was the point of disembarkation, and we found a seedy hotel for the night.

The next day we boarded a bus to Lake Toba. On the way, the bus stopped to allow those Muslims who wished, to get off and visit a mosque for one of their daily prayers. Opposite the mosque was a sign announcing "Texas English School," and we wandered across to see what it was all about. Immediately a teacher and students wishing to practice their English engaged us in conversation. Before we knew it, we were inside giving an English lesson to a class full of students! In the time it takes to say the Moslem prayers, we had given our first lesson and put Canada on the map in a small village in Sumatra. Friendly waves sent us on our way towards Lake Toba.

Lake Toba is a crater lake with a large island in the centre, truly a beautiful scene. A small ferry took us to the island where we rented a motorbike for a tour of the island. It is a great way to explore and we left the "main" road to travel mud paths into a rarely visited village. There we were surrounded by curious children anxious to touch us and communicate however they could. We passed through an area where sulphur smells emanated from the still active volcanic rocks. The road became rougher and, finally, a wide river blocked our path. It had been a year of heavy rains and the road had been washed away, so we had to abort our circumnavigation of the island and return the way we had come. We had explored Samosir Island on a day trip and could have spent longer but we had used up relaxing time on the other island of Ko Chang in Thailand.

The next day we joined a group of travellers to share a minibus. There was an English couple, an Australian doctor called Adam, Kees and Louanne from Saskatoon, Saskatchewan, and a couple of Germans who didn't talk much. We headed south towards the equator through spectacular countryside with endless views over thick green jungles and raging rivers.

All was fine until the rains started. The roads disintegrated before our eyes. Our driver was driving crazily for the conditions. We learned later that he had killed a soldier on the road the night before and somehow talked his way out of jail to make his return trip. The bus windows leaked and I got wet and cold. We came to know all our fellow travellers very well in our shared adversity. The journey slowed and our discomfort increased as the road worsened. We cheered ourselves by singing and playing our cassette tapes. Noreen put her earphones in her ears to take her mind off her surroundings and what she thought was imminent death.

It became dark outside. We were supposed to have crossed the equator in daylight but it was midnight when we finally reached the white line across the road marking the demarcation of hemispheres. It was still raining in torrents but we all piled out to jump back and forth like idiots across the white line, just to say we had crossed the equator many times. Some of us stood on either side of the line and kissed. We were in the middle of nowhere at midnight, but the tee shirt vendors appeared out of the darkness and sold some of their wares to the crazy tourists. Later that night, after a seventeen-hour bus journey through hell, we collapsed into comfortable beds in the town of Bukittinggi and slept for twelve hours, only interrupted once at four o'clock by the call to prayer from the mosque just outside our window.

Bukittinggi is a market town with streets filled with every kind of merchandise imaginable. The exotic fruits were plentiful, as were the live eels, fishes, snakes and bats. Medicine men and snake oil salesmen provided entertainment. We were given a guided tour by two sari-clad Moslem schoolgirls who practised their English while pointing out the interesting foods for a couple of hours. At the end they invited us back to their village to meet their family. It was a generous invitation, and one we would have liked to accept, but it meant another long bus ride and that would have been too much for us after our previous day's ordeal.

We saw a show of traditional dancing in the evening, and the following day, set out to visit the caves carved by Javanese prisoners in the Second World War for storage of Japanese munitions. From there we walked to the mini Grand Canyon of Bukittinggi where we met a botany student who explained the fauna and flora of the area. He stayed with us for hours and led us through rivers to wonderfully cooling swimming pools and then to the daytime resting places of enormous fruit bats, also known as flying foxes. We climbed the canyon wall to his village, which is renowned for its silver filigree. An artist sold us some of his exquisite work. Night was drawing near and, in the fading light, hundreds of flying foxes blackened the sky further with their six-foot wingspans. This was a threatening sight for those afraid of bats but a wondrous one for Noreen who is fascinated by them for some reason.

By now, visibility was poor to none and we still had the canyon to re-cross. Fortunately our unofficial guide was still with us and took us down narrow, slippery trails through the jungle and canyon walls towards a single distant light. We had to keep a hand on each other's shoulders to stay with him. At one point, a cow startled us as we brushed past it in the darkness but we were successfully guided back to town. There, our guide disappeared into the darkness, refusing any reward for giving us a unique experience that could not have been purchased.

A bus took us to Padang the following day where we arranged to fly to Java. At the airport we ran into Kees, Louanne and Adam, with whom we had survived the harrowing bus trip and remembered the hell we had recently shared. It was the first of several times that we accidentally ran into members of that bonded group in different parts of South-East Asia. It is a small world, as they say.

Java

We spent only a short time on the island of Java. I was under the weather while we were in Jakarta and Noreen had a cold during our stay in Yogyakarta. But we managed some sightseeing in each place, and the highlights for me were the docks in Jakarta and the Buddhist temple of Borobudur.

The Jakarta docks struck me for the rows of fishing boats with high, sloping bows, typical of that part of the world. On the train to Yogja, we shared the journey with the vice-president of Indonesia and his entourage. We even used his red carpet to enter and leave the train.

Borobudur is a magnificent temple of over four hundred Buddhas staring out of open chambers; another seventy sit behind latticed stupas. The whole site commands fabulous views over the surrounding countryside. I reached it easily by motorcycle from Yogja and enjoyed the ride through lovely, tropical green scenery, and small villages. It was similar to the scenery from the train that had taken us from Jakarta to Yogja.

The next stop on our tour was the island of Bali. We decided to fly, rather than take a combination of buses, trains and boats. We were anxious to spend as much time on that magical island of Bali before our two-month Indonesian visa ran out.

Rice Terraces, Central Bali, Indonesia

Chapter 3

Island of the Gods

The Merpati Airline's turbo-prop aircraft approached the main airport for Bali, flying over Kuta Beach, just outside the capital, Denpasar.

We made our way by taxi to Kuta and checked into a bungalow development away from the madding crowds of Jalan Legian, the main street. It was a true oasis from the hundreds of street pedlars who hassle you throughout Kuta. The town itself is thronged with Australians who fly in on charter flights every day to party until they drop. Kuta had been a small sleepy place until surfers discovered the fabulous sandy beaches with waves to die for. The beach is still breathtaking and extends for miles, but the section near Kuta and Legian is well populated and patrolled by the ever-present merchants selling sarongs, watches and jewellery or offering massages. These days they are kept at the top of the beach but you still have to push through them to reach the sand.

Kuta is the only place where you will see topless sunbathing which the Aussies love to do. The Balinese Hindu population frowns upon such behaviour normally but put up with it for the sake of the Australian dollars flowing into their coffers. Kuta is a great place to shop but you have to be prepared to bargain items down to about half the starting price. The batik fabrics are beautiful, and the carvings and artwork most attractive. Don't be put off by the numbers of almost identical hand-carved objects, when you arrive home, they look twice as striking in isolation. The hours of work put into them translate to an hourly wage of less than a dollar a day for the price you pay for them.

South of Kuta are the tourist zones of Nusa Dua and Sanur. The former is a special up-market government organized area with international, first class hotels on manicured, guarded beaches where you would go as rich independent or package tourists intent on getting a tan in a week. Not the real Bali. Sanur is more of a mixture of traditional Balinese hotels and fancier newer imports. The golden sand beach is spectacular. At the extreme south point of Bali the temple of Ulu Watu stands precariously on the edge of a cliff with waves crashing onto ragged rocks hundreds of feet below. It is well worth a visit.

Moving East from Kuta, you drive through the stone carving village of Batubulan. Dozens of workshops line the road and carvers, young and old, practise their trade, oblivious to the tourists who stop to watch. It is best to walk to the back of the shops where the real work is done. The stone used on Bali is soft and easy to carve, but the problem is that it equally easily erodes with the wind and rain. This means that carvings don't last many years in the environment and have to be replaced periodically. Beneficially, the tradition of carving is continued through generations as the stone carvings are important to the Balinese for their thousands of temples and family compounds. Every town you pass has a stone entry and exit carving, every family compound has stone shrines to their ancestors, and every temple has its stone statues.

Not far from Batubulan is the village of Celuk, known for its silver and gold work. Again there are many workshops carrying out similar work and the tour buses stop at the more expensive, fancy showrooms where one or two artists carry out perfunctory activities for the sake of the tourists. The real work is done in the back streets. Further north is the village of Mas where woodcarving is their forte. The most expensive works are made from sweet smelling sandalwood and you usually have to ask for the special cabinet holding it to be opened for you. Mas is very close to Ubud, the artisan capital of Bali and a centre from which to tour East and North Bali. We made it our base for ten days on our first trip to Bali and have returned to it on every subsequent visit.

Ubud

Ubud is a bustling town geared for tourists, yet it is quite different from Kuta. It attracts artists from around the world, many of whom have made it their home. The outstanding beauty and tranquillity of the surrounding countryside doubtless provides inspiration for their work.

Terraced rice fields surround Ubud, their green and gold crops ever changing as three crops a year are taken from them. The engineering of the irrigation schemes has to be marvelled at and has been developed over generations. The wood and mud sluice gate arrangements have been somewhat modified with concrete and steel parts added, but the management of the water is still done by consultation between the farmers who tend their fields with manual labour only. The only help they get is from the working ducks that eat the pests, and cultivate and fertilize the soil at the same time.

A walk through the rice fields is a must in Bali and always a free highlight of any trip there. Day trips by tourist bus or motorbike are good ways to discover the secrets of Bali, and Ubud is well placed for anyone to arrange them. We have explored many back roads and trails in the mountains and along the coasts and we never fail to come across a temple ceremony going on somewhere. Invariably we are invited to take pictures as we witness ceremonies that continue the tradition of centuries. We were invited to join in a picnic on one occasion--the only foreigners among five hundred Balinese on a beach on the north coast. The Balinese are a special, gentle people with strong spiritual beliefs. They preserve their traditions and lifestyles and are not influenced much by the Western tourists who have been coming to their island for decades.

The drive north and east of Ubud takes you around two active volcanoes, Gunung Batur and Gunung Agung. Major eruptions have occurred within living memory on several occasions and many lives have been lost and homes destroyed. It is no surprise, therefore, that the Balinese have great respect for the mountain gods and have built huge temples on their hillsides. The largest such temple is Besakih, the mother temple, which is always teeming with worshippers and tourists alike. It is indubitably impressive but its beauty is taken away by the avenue of trinket shops that line the approach, and by the persistent pedlars who impede your every step. We usually visit the somewhat smaller Kehen temple in Bangli, early in the morning before other tourists arrive, and enjoy it more than Besakih.

A visit to Bali is incomplete without seeing a cremation ceremony. This is a time to celebrate the life of the deceased and is not a sad occasion. The coffin and offerings are paraded through the town or village to the local temple of the dead, accompanied by scores, sometimes hundreds, of friends, relatives and neighbours. They bang gongs and swing the coffin in wild circles to confuse any evil spirits who may be trying to follow the body to the cremation. We have seen four cremations, all different from each other--some for the rich and some for the poor. Sometimes the poor will bury their dead until they have enough money for a cremation, or until they can share the cost by joining in with other families for a cremation of several people together. Then they dig up the bodies for the ceremony.

A story I like to tell concerns one of our explorations by motorbike, when we became lost in north Bali. We had a fairly detailed map that we thought we had followed carefully and which would have led us over a mountain range, back to Ubud. The road was paved initially, then unpaved; a grass strip appeared in the centre before it deteriorated into a mud path. Undaunted, we pressed on, up ever increasing grades in muddy terrain until Noreen fell off the back of the bike. She gamely remounted and was promptly thrown off again, as the hill became steeper. The third time she fell off, I fell off too and it was time to reassess the situation. We didn't have time to retrace our route, as it would have been dark before we got back and, in any case, the path would be even more slippery and dangerous to drive down. We decided to press on, walking alongside the bike until I lost all control of it and we had to give up. We were in a pickle.

Out of the bush came a wiry old man carrying a huge bale of rice and he assessed our predicament in a flash. He dropped his load of rice, picked up the bike and pushed it effortlessly up the slippery slope about a quarter of a mile to the plateau above. He beckoned us to get on and, refusing any payment, set off down the hill to pick up his own load again. We continued our journey to a deserted, tiny hamlet that had a Coca-Cola sign over a small shop. For a fraction of what we would pay in Ubud, the owner sold us a warm pop, and within minutes the hamlet became alive with children and adults rushing in to see the strangers. White people very rarely, if ever, find this village. We reached Ubud half an hour before dark with warm feelings for that stranger who helped us because he wanted to, and for the Balinese who welcomed us to their village.

Candidasa

Candidasa is a beach town, built for the tourist trade around a fishing village. As we were checking into one of the standard hotels on the beach strip, we again bumped into Kees and Louanne whom we had met twice in Sumatra and once in Java. We only had a short time to catch up with their news but knew that we would see them again in Canada in six months.

Unfortunately, much of the coral reef in front of Candidasa was used to make the concrete for hotels and bridges. Loss of the reef caused loss of the beaches and to try to encourage the sand to return, huge berms and breakwaters were built. These are somewhat unsightly and Candidasa has never developed in the way it was planned. We like it though, as it has all the conveniences without the people. Snorkelling around offshore islets is remarkable and small dugout canoes with outriggers can take you to wonderful beaches nearby where you can have a mile of white sand to yourself.

Excursions you can take from Candidasa include a visit to Tenganan, a traditional village inhabited by one of the first peoples who came to Bali. It is a walled village, particularly known for its *double ikat* weaving method. The village may be reached by road direct from Candidasa but a more interesting route takes you on a roundabout pathway through rice fields and across a river, so that you approach Tenganan from the north through a jungle area. You would have to find a local guide to take you. Another daytrip is to the water palace near the town of Amlapura; it is a favourite place for locals rather than tourists. The marketplace in Amlapura is also worth a visit and to complete your day, you can head north and east to some of the most beautiful terraced rice fields on the island in Tirtagangga.

We stayed in Dewa Bharata Bungalows, one of the standard hotels on the strip of main road through Candidasa. All the hotels are quite small and are run by

Balinese. The exception to this Amankila, an exclusive hotel, a few miles out that caters to the rich and famous. This intrigued us, so we set off one day to walk down the coast to catch a glimpse of how the other half of the world lives. We were halted by a massive rock stretching vertically from the sea and came across a group of local children playing nearby. They verified that the hotel we were looking for was around the rock and showed us how we could climb around it, giving us needed assistance. As we rounded the rocks, we spotted an armed guard in a speedboat off a beautifully groomed, sandy beach. Deckchairs were neatly laid out and a few white bodies lay on them. Ignoring the guard, we walked along the beach pretending we knew where we were going, nodding at the rich and famous as we passed. We found a quiet area at the end of the beach and enjoyed the picnic we had brought and took a swim.

At the end of the day, we plucked up the courage to visit the hotel proper and entered the toilets and change rooms. Large fluffy towels tempted Noreen to take a shower and make herself presentable. Suitably groomed, we marched smartly to the reception area and asked to be shown around. We saw magnificent villas in private gardens with their own swimming pool. The focal point was a huge lounging area near a large pool. The blue pool had a weir on the sea side, giving the swimmers a view clear to the horizon. It was a fabulous hotel in a fantastic location but we could not have afforded even breakfast. It would have blown our budget for a week. Heads held high, we thanked the manager who had shown us around, walked down the long driveway to the road and hitchhiked back to our modest but clean and comfortable hotel.

We made several friends in Candidasa and have kept in touch with them over the years. Ayu and Wayan were waitresses in Dewa Bharata Bungalows and were paid about a dollar a day for their labours. On our first visit they were both single and sharing cramped accommodation in the hotel. Now they are both married and sharing cramped accommodation with their husbands and children, but they live in separate houses. Ayu is a beautiful lady who has had a hard life. When she married, she had to move into her husband's family compound and found it difficult to work with her mother-in-law who was very demanding. Ayu now has a new job in a shop in Kuta and somehow manages to look after her husband and two children. She has been sick with typhoid but struggles on. We try to see her every time we visit Bali and help her a little financially. Wayan still works in Candidasa and probably will stay there for her whole life.

On Whitesand Beach, which can only be reached by boat, we met another Balinese person whom we have seen on most of our trips. His name was Nengar Sanar and he had learned English by listening to the radio from Australia and came up to us to practice it. He invited us to see his family compound and showed us his outdoor kitchen and primitive sleeping rooms. His job was in an expensive diving resort in East Bali where he worked in the laundry. We were horrified to see that Nengar slept on the ironing board when he stayed in the resort during the week. At weekends, he stayed in the family home so he could help his mother in the rice fields. We wrote a letter to the resort suggesting that our friend would be better employed in a public area where his English and interpersonal skills could be used. Nengar was moved to the bar area but it meant working longer hours and he could not get time off to return home to work in the fields. Consequently he is back at work in the laundry.

Lovely Lombok

Lombok is the island to the east of Bali and is easily reached from Candidasa by a ferry from Padang Bai. A predominately Moslem fishing village, Padang Bai is in a natural harbour where the ferries dock. Unfortunately the old ferry-boats pollute the long, curved sandy beach. A half-mile away on the other side is a lovely smaller bay that had a few shacks set back from the beach when we were first there, but now people have discovered the gorgeous beach and more substantial buildings have appeared.

One day we were there, I was swimming in the crystal clear waters when I spotted a leather wallet floating by; it turned out to be mine. Embarrassed at my carelessness, I laid out the huge numbers of rupiah to dry on the logs at the top of the beach. A while later, a rogue wave came in and washed all the money into the sea. Seeing the sea of money, local children who had been watching us, dived into the water to retrieve the scores of bank notes. I thought that I had just donated about a hundred dollars to the local economy when I saw the children laying out my money on the grass behind the beach. Each bank note had a small stone on it to stop it blowing away. I did not lose a Rupiah.

The ferry we took to Lombok was a high-speed catamaran, which took about two hours for the crossing. Unfortunately it came on hard economic times and now the only ferries are the old clunkers which crawl across in three or four hours. During the crossing we admired the views of the beaches and volcano Gunung Agung and were escorted part of the way by a school of dolphins which played in our bow wave. At the ferry terminal in Lembar on Lombok, we found our Perama minivan, which whisked us off to the tourist area of Senggigi Beach. Perama is a large company that has fleets of vans providing regularly scheduled shuttles all over Bali and Lombok.

The whole east coast of Lombok is blessed with glorious, untouched empty beaches. The only exception is Senggigi, where there are services for tourists to attract the travellers who make that little bit of effort needed to leave Bali. It is worth the effort to see the difference between the island cultures, one Hindu, the other Moslem. An excellent way to discover the secrets of Lombok is to rent a motorbike, and we did that on several days. It is easy to get off the beaten track and see the Sasak weaving and pottery villages from the back roads.

After a particularly hot drive oneday, we came across an empty mosque on the edge of a village. There was no one around so we lay down on the cool marble floor to rest awhile. In just a few minutes, the word was out that two strangers were in town and we became surrounded by curious women and children wanting to talk to us and touch us. I entertained them by showing pictures of them on my video camera.

The drive through the middle to the north coast of Lombok took us through groves of Durian trees and the pungent fruit was in season. You know it is in season by the smell from a mile away. Noreen tried it and loved it. I didn't try it and hated it from a distance. The road reaches a ridge and descends through a forest full of monkeys. I have never seen anything like it--literally hundreds of the friendly animals in sight for several miles. Before we hit the coast we passed through fields of peanuts and rice. They were flat, not like the terraced fields of Bali. The north coast climate is dry, being shielded by the massive form of Mount Ringani, an active volcano and the second highest mountain in Indonesia. Somehow the villagers scrape a living from the soil; one of the crops there is cashew nut.

There are several ancient villages in the area. We were exploring a trail up a dry riverbed when we discovered one of them. I won't tell you the name, as I don't want anyone else to find it. There was no electricity or running water and the village was totally surrounded by a high fence. The houses were in perfect rows and the mud "streets" were swept clean. People have lived there that way for centuries without the influence of outsiders; it is an anthropologist's delight.

The villagers invited us into the compound and into their homes where we saw primitive kitchens and utensils and simple sleeping arrangements. We saw them weaving palm leaves and drying tapioca. They had seen photographs and cameras before but they had never before seen themselves on videotape. I felt guilty after showing the headman but he was very enthusiastic and asked me to show the children too. They laughed a lot! On a subsequent visit, we took a pair of binoculars, which was also a first. Some of the villagers were frightened to see objects magically come closer.

There is an ancient village at Senaru. It is the starting point for treks to the summit of mount Ringani but has been ruined by the scores of hikers passing by. Handouts of money have left the villagers idle, and all they seem to do is smoke and chew betel nuts, which leaves them in a perpetually drugged state. Near Senaru there is a really high waterfall and we revelled in its cool, drenching, powerful torrent of fresh water.

Off the north-west corner of Lombok lie three islands: Gili Air, Gili Meno and Gili Trawangan. We decided to check out Gili Meno as we had heard that it was a little quieter than Gili Trawangan, which is popular with the younger crowd. We took one of the regular ferries from Bangsal and it dropped us on the beach in front of one of several beach bungalow developments. All the bungalows on the beach were occupied so we found a rustic hut a hundred yards back from the beach. It turned out to be very hot at night and there was no electricity on the island so there were no fans either. We found it difficult to sleep and got up frequently to sponge ourselves with tepid salt water. All the water came from a shallow well under a salt-water lake in the centre of the island.

We arose early and watched a magnificent sunrise over Mount Ringani. After breakfast we walked all around the island; it took us a whole hour. The beach was white sand littered with shells; on the west side there were waves and on the east it was dead calm. We spent the day lazing in the shade of trees and dropped into the sea for a swim every hour. The snorkelling was wonderful in the shallows and an underwater wall which dropped from the shallows a hundred yards out, allowed the big fish to come and check us out.

It was truly a desert island paradise. We braved the hot nights and even became used to them, but we really enjoyed days of total relaxation, reading, swimming, walking and doing nothing. I cannot remember how long we stayed there.

We returned to civilization, as it were, just north of Senggigi Beach at the small village of Mangset. The accommodation was called Windy Beach Cottages but I am not sure if it was ever windy on the beach; the owner's name, however, was Windy. She was a Balinese princess who had been expelled from Bali by her family for marrying a Scotsman. The cottages were lovely and we gradually came out of our total relaxation mode by making trips into the resort of Senggigi.

Eventually we returned to Candidasa, Bali to celebrate Christmas and the New Year. Dewa Bharata, our hotel in Candidasa, was a second home to us and we became firm friends with the staff and came to know all the guests too. We partied at a different restaurant every night over the holiday period. The hotel staff asked our advice about a New Year party and roasted a pig and put on a Balinese dance show. There was a strange mixture of gamelan music and Christmas carols but somehow it worked in the tropical environment endowing it with the spirituality of both Hinduism and Christianity.

We left Indonesia on the day our visa expired, or so we thought. Actually we were a day late by immigration calculations and were pulled aside for interrogation. After a suitable reprimand we were let go and allowed to board our flight to Perth, Western Australia.

On the plane Noreen started to run a fever and during our first night in Perth, it worsened to a very high temperature with severe shivers. Concerned, we headed for a hospital, where she was admitted and underwent several blood tests. By then, the fever had dropped below the optimum point to determine if she had malaria. Finally, after treatment and a battery of all kinds of tests, she was released from hospital and told she had probably picked up a mosquito borne virus on Lombok. During the time Noreen was hospitalized, I had some time to explore Perth and came to like it very much. This is described in the chapter on Australia.

Singapore--No Chewing Gum Here

Finally it was time to start heading north again, as we still had to visit Singapore and Malaysia. Our first stop was Singapore and we headed to the post office where we had a post restante address. It was like Christmas in February with all the mail we had received from our friends back home. The Singapore post office had a grand hall with easy chairs for reading and chairs and tables for writing--it was well set up for travellers. The city-state is organized with effectiveness. Lots of new high rise office buildings and hotels mingle with attractive older Chinese and British Colonial structures.

The streets are kept immaculately clean and there are severe penalties for dropping used chewing gum on the sidewalks. Our time in the city was short and we did a lot of walking, as well as riding a high gondola to a recreation area on an island near the port. There was a huge and lovely Butterfly Park in a conservatory where I admired insects I had never seen before. It brought back memories of collecting butterflies in England when I was a boy.

When I think of Singapore, I mostly remember the shops and the fabulous foods we ate. The outdoor food stalls in Newton served wonderful concoctions from the various ethnic communities that make up Singapore and Malaysia.

One evening we arranged to have a pre-dinner drink with a friend of a friend from Vancouver. She was a senior executive at a five star hotel, and we met her in her hotel lounge. We got on very well, so well in fact that she invited us to be her guest for dinner in their exclusive restaurant. You can dress us up and take us anywhere so we accepted, and enjoyed a sumptuous meal with wine, which I shall remember for a long time.

Raffles Hotel is one of the places to see and be seen in Singapore. It is horrendously expensive but you must try a Singapore Sling in their famous bar. The whole hotel is renovated beautifully to its original colonial splendour. After your expensive drink, you can cross the street to that famous Scottish restaurant, McDonald's, and buy an ice cream.

Peninsular Malaysia

We took a bus from Singapore to the Malaysian border and another bus up the coast to Malacca, an old, Portuguese colonial town that had been taken over by the British and then the Japanese before becoming part of the new Malaysia after the war. We used the normal trishaw method of travel in the town and visited an interesting Chinese temple, enjoyed a curry on a banana leaf in an Indian restaurant, and attended a Portuguese show in the old part of town, a mile down the coast. There we were introduced to a Portuguese couple, Joe and Isabel from Vancouver, and spent a very pleasant evening together. Next we visited friends in the capital, Kuala Lumpur, where we stayed a few days and did some sightseeing. The butterfly farm again attracted my attention and I took more close-up videos of the colourful insects.

We continued up the coast and took a ferry to the island of Pulau Pangkor, just offshore. We were looking around a small hotel to check on their rooms when we ran into Joe and Isabel again; we had no idea they were even headed that way. Naturally, we spent more time with them and subsequently got together with them in Vancouver. We also met them in Costa Rica a few years later.

There were small boats to rent and we took one to a smaller island where we had to chase the monkeys off a beach so that we could have exclusive use of the idyllic scene. After swimming, we were looking at the blue waters when the surface was suddenly broken by the head of a large sea snake, which gave us a deadly gaze. A sea snake is extremely poisonous and I suppose we were lucky not to have run into it when we were swimming. I threw in a rock and it quickly disappeared. It was so hot on the beach that we were desperate for another swim to cool off. I took the precaution of throwing in another rock to scare the snake and, sure enough, he had been lurking in the shallows waiting for us. We took a very short cooling swim and rowed back to Pulau Pangkor, we were not going to compete for space in the environment of a sea snake.

We returned to the mainland and caught a train to Butterworth, from which there is a ferry to Penang. There was a bridge under construction nearby and doubtless it is now in use. We continued the tour of Georgetown that we had started several months earlier and took a funicular railway to a vantage spot high above the town. We noticed several fancy villas built by the British colonialists during their rule; they knew how to live in style.

It was nearing the end of our trip and we were starting to wonder how everything and everyone at home was doing. There was no readily accessible e-mail in those days and we had been out of touch for months. The train took us north to the border with Thailand where the engines were changed and it continued on to Bangkok. We rested at our familiar Borarn House hotel overnight and flew on to Hong Kong. We had originally planned to carry straight on to Vancouver, but our new friends in Hong Kong had persuaded us to spend another week with them on the way home. This we did and saw even more of the large territory that was to be handed back by the British to the Chinese a few years later. We did our final shopping for souvenirs and presents and said good-bye to Asia, knowing we would return soon.

Noreen, Ayu & son in Puri Saraswati, Ubud, Bali

Sunset over Gunung Agung Volcano, Bali

Ancient Village, Lombok, Indonesia

Author with Rafflesia Flower, Gunung Gading Park, Sarawak, Borneo

Tunku Abdul Rahman Park near Kota Kinabalu, Sabah, Borneo

Chapter 4

Bali, Banda and Borneo Bound

Back to Beautiful Bali

When Noreen and I returned home from Asia, our travel agent asked us which place we had enjoyed the most. We replied, in unison, "Bali." The agent then suggested we return and take a group with us so that we could get a free air ticket from the airline. We thought about it briefly and it sounded a little like hard work. After all, weren't we retired?

Almost two years later, we thought about the idea again and realized that it might not be too difficult to put a tour together. Noreen had kept a journal that included all the places where we had stayed. The highlights of our stay on Bali were still very much in our minds. It would be great to go back. I had hours of videos that I could edit into a promotional video, which would show any prospective client exactly where they would be staying, and the sights they would be seeing. We wrote to the hotels and obtained favourable group rates. Our travel agent contacted Garuda, the Indonesian national airline, and they offered us one free ticket and a good group rate if we bought ten tickets.

To publicize our trip, we posted signs headed "Beautiful Bali on a Budget" in travel shops, coffee shops and any community notice board we could find. We told all our friends and even took out one advertisement in the Vancouver Sun newspaper. I wrote an article for the local free newspaper and they published it with photos I had taken on our trip. Actually, one of the photos wasn't of Bali at all, it was of Noreen on a beach in Thailand, but no one knew the difference. The word of our tour got around and we were soon taking deposits from customers. It was just two weeks before we were due to leave and we were still one short of the required number of paying seats to get our free one. Fortunately, Tom and Bev, whom we knew slightly from the Wobbley Wheelers, decided that it would be a good time for them to take a break, and we had our full complement with one spare.

Members of our first group ranged in age from eighteen to fifty nine and came from many different backgrounds; some were singles, some couples. We introduced them to each other at a wine and cheese party in our home, and it was obvious that they would get along well together. The most asked question from people was "How long is the flight?" to which I replied I didn't know. I explained that it was too complicated to calculate since we were crossing the date line. I knew of course, but I was reluctant to tell them it was as long as it was.

The flight was interrupted by a refuelling stop in Hawaii and the "shy" member of the group started doing a dance routine in the holding lounge. It also happened to be my birthday. The birthday would only last for a few hours as we were crossing the date line west of Hawaii. The group all sang "Happy Birthday" and Noreen distributed a Terry's chocolate orange to celebrate. We were off to a positive start, although it would be a long flight.

The tour went well for the ten days in Kuta and Ubud and then Candidasa. Everyone was getting on well and the excursions had worked out with no transportation problems. We had a tour planned for every other day, leaving lots of free time for the group to explore on their own, while all evenings were free too. Actually the group decided to eat together each evening, and they shared their experiences and adventures of the day.

On the day of our big tour of the island past the volcanoes, we had arranged for two mini-vans. We had picked up three intrepid members of the group who had climbed Gunung Batur for the sunrise and had started to make our way to the north coast. We were attracted to a crowd around the temple in Kintamani and stopped the vans to take some pictures. I was so intent on that video moment that I failed to see a missing manhole cover in the sidewalk and plunged into the hole, cutting my shin to the bone, dislocating my shoulder and ruining my camera. The group rushed to my aid, Noreen bandaged my leg temporarily and I was transported to the closest hospital. Some of the activity was captured on film for posterity. I tried to get one van to continue the tour without me but the group was too upset and returned to Candidasa to await the return of their leader.

Meanwhile at the hospital, the doctor produced a tray of rusty instruments and started to unwrap my bandages. Noreen soon put a stop to that and I was carried off, in some pain I should add, to another hospital, miles away in Gianyar. It was much bigger and slightly cleaner, if one didn't look up as I was doing from my horizontal position. The doctor produced some fishing line sitting in alcohol and again, Noreen stopped him to ask for sterile suture material. There being none, she set off to a pharmacy to try to find some, but without success. After a further search in the hospital, some soluble sutures were found; they were not really suitable for holding my shin together but at least they were sterile. I had been drugged and fortunately was feeling little pain as they sewed me up, also using steristrips from our own first aid kit.

The whole operation was recorded on videotape by one of the group! I was lucky to have Noreen and my daughter, Pippa, alongside me during my ordeal; they were a great comfort.

After the operation, which cost almost nothing, I was feeling fine but it was obviously too late to continue our tour of the island. Instead our driver took us to his village where we met his family and held court in his compound while supping cool drinks. Finally we returned to our hotel where a very sober group were waiting for us. They had been worried that their leader would be out of commission and they would have been unable to complete their trip. They need not have worried though: I would not be swimming during the trip, but all activities would be carried out according to the published itinerary.

We did have three other small medical problems with members of the group but again they had little impact on the tour. The first casualty was Bev whose lips were sunburned in a swimming pool. She had not followed the advice given during our pre-tour briefing and had neglected her sunscreen; it put a cramp in her love life but didn't stop her getting engaged to Tom on Lombok

A near disaster occurred when another lady tried to chew the betel nut concoction at an ancient village on Lombok. Her throat immediately swelled and she had difficulty breathing; it was a violent allergic reaction. Fortunately one member of the group, Sadru, had some anti-histamine with him and applied it to her tongue, causing the reaction to subside.

The last problem involved Sadru experiencing some heart palpitations that caused him to forego two nights on the remote island of Gili Meno, which is far from medical help. Now we ask all our clients to declare any known potential problems that may affect their participation in our tours, and we get them to sign a waiver to that effect.

The group became pretty close and seemed to enjoy themselves. When we returned to Kuta Beach on our last night, Helen, a girl travelling alone, met us. She had heard from someone about our group having a good time and she wanted to find out what we had been doing. Helen ended up joining our group for dinner and fitted right in. At the dinner, two of the group had organized awards for participants and we had lots of fun talking about each other. Tom received the award for contributing most towards the Indonesian economy. He had bought about twenty tee-shirts, a dozen watches, some large wooden carvings and much, much more. Tom had also bought a huge bag in which to carry his purchases home. Bali is a fantastic place for excellent presents at bargain prices, and it was only a few weeks before Christmas. All the awards were very personal and tailored to the recipients, giving everyone a good feeling about our holiday together.

We sent out a questionnaire after we returned home and received useful positive feedback. That enabled us to improve our package of activities on future tours. The success of that first group encouraged us to organize more trips; we had not been at all certain that leading groups would be as much fun. We gave ourselves the name "Hot Tours," printed some business cards and took out an e-mail address: hot_tours@hotmail.com. It is important in Indonesia to have a title such as "Tour Leader" or "Tour Manager" and to have cards to give out--they lead to bigger discounts!

We made some changes to our itinerary for the next trip, and this kept the tour fresh while also incorporating clients' input. The hotels we stay in change slightly each year as we discover better ones, and as we are able to bargain a little harder with bigger groups. In order to get our free ticket, we now have to have fifteen paid tickets, and this is using Malaysian Airlines, as Garuda Airlines no longer flies to North America.

Each of our groups is different and the interpersonal relationships could be a thesis subject for a psychologist. It would be unfair for me to write about it, even if I changed the names to protect the guilty. Nearly all the people in our groups keep in touch with one another after their trips and have the occasional reunion to share the good times again. Some of us have become really good friends and see lots of each other. We have come to know people all over the world and we enjoy visiting them in their homes and entertaining them in our home in Vancouver.

The first group was all very saddened when they heard that Tom had died of cancer just over two years later. There had been close bonding with the big man who had got so much out of the trip by becoming engaged, buying so much and helping everyone to have the best of times. The word of our group has travelled far and wide, and we now have clients from all over the United States, Honduras and Canada and even interest from the United Kingdom. All this sounds like a commercial for Hot Tours doesn't it? Actually we don't want to do more than one trip a year, or it will become a job and start to interfere with our retirement!

Birthdays and anniversaries have been celebrated on our tours and we usually create a unique event that we all remember for a long time. A recent fiftieth anniversary of a couple from Wisconsin involved organizing exclusive use of a restaurant with exotic drinks, a band to play golden oldies and a gaudy cake. The cake was made in a neighbouring village and brought to the party on a motorbike. It was beautifully decorated with real orchids and a huge "50" candle. The restaurant was decorated with sweet smelling flowers and the whole evening was a moving experience for us all. Several people have made repeat tours with us and several have gained the confidence to continue the tour on their own by flying on to Australia, Malaysia and Borneo after our tours.

We are frequently asked if we have a specific focus to our tours. We don't, actually, but we have had

dancers, potters, weavers, photographers and bird
watchers with us at different times. All these people
found their special interests well looked after. Most of
our people are considerate of the rest of the group and
follow our leadership and suggestions. One exception
was when two sisters decided to come together on a trip.
They shared a room and neglected to put their valuables
in the hotel safe. They also neglected to close their
balcony door. The result was the loss of a passport,
money and a pair of $4000, diamond-studded earrings.
The police reports and interviews took up hours of
precious time and they were lucky to get their
replacement passport in time to return to Canada with the
group.

The Banda Islands and Spices

We have taken advantage of our tours by going on to
other places after the group has gone home. Actually,
Sadru and Farida, who came to Bali with us on our first
group tour, also came on our second tour. They continued
to travel with Noreen and I after the group had returned
home. We had originally planned to visit the islands of
Nusa Tenggara, just east of Bali. The first of these is
Lombok, followed by Sumbawa, Flores and Timor. In
between are scores of smaller islands, the most famous
being Komodo Island, home of the Komodo dragons.
When we were in the area, there was considerable unrest
in East Timor due to a strong independence movement.
This resulted in all out-war a few years later.

Instead, we overflew Nusa Tenggara and visited the islands further east, known as the Spice Islands. Beautiful photographs and descriptions of the Spice Islands had appeared in *Escape* magazine a week before we had left on our trip. We really had to check them out for ourselves.

We booked our flights in Bali and received tickets and reservations via Sulawesi and Ambon to the Banda Islands. We reached Ambon and were to stay only one day before flying on to Banda Neira, the principal island of the Banda Islands. It was fortunate that we confirmed our flight as soon as we arrived in Ambon, since the airline office had no record of our onward reservations. All flights to Banda Neira are booked manually by one individual who carefully writes each name on his list. There were only two or three flights a week on a twenty-seater aircraft but they would only carry fifteen passengers, as the runway on Banda Neira is very short.

A further complication was that only twelve passengers could be flown off the island at a time as the runway sloped steeply to the ocean and it would be dangerous to carry more. We were told that there were no seats available for three days and we booked ourselves on the next available flight. Sadru and Farida had only limited time and were fortunate to take the seats of a couple who had even less time available. The couple had a flight to Banda Neira but could not fly off the island in time to catch their connecting flight home to Holland. We said good-bye to Sadru and Farida and spent the following days exploring Ambon and the island of Saparua.

We spent a very hot night and two days on Saparua where we walked and bussed around the whole island.

There is an interesting Dutch fort with cannons facing a peaceful sea and a pottery village where they mould pots without the use of a wheel. Snorkelling is quite good but not as good as on Gili Meno. The island residents were curious and friendly but the only two other tourists were not. We ran into them several times but they seemed preoccupied, and we thought that their English might not be too good. We guessed that they were German and tried to engage them in conversation but could not. We saw them again later back in Ambon and in Banda Neira, and it turned out that they had been ill in Saparua. They subsequently became firm friends and we travelled with them to the Kei Islands.

In Ambon City on Ambon Island, we visited a huge cemetery, which held the graves of thousands of allied soldiers who had died at the hands of the Japanese when they swept through the island in the Second World War. It is a beautiful tropical garden, immaculately cared for by the locals who are paid by the Australian Government. Ambon has suffered occupation by Portuguese and Dutch colonialists and been governed by British, Australian and Japanese. The city was mainly destroyed when it was bombed by the allies during the war. It has undergone internal strife for centuries. The island is half Christian and half Moslem and even now they are fighting each other. There is a strong movement to be independent from Indonesia as well.

The day came for our flight to the Banda Islands and we waited at the airport for hours. One plane left and there were still a few passengers remaining but we were assured that the plane would return for us. We met an interesting American lady, Vana, who was a teacher at the International School in Jakarta. She was visiting the

Bandas to check out facilities for a school trip. Vana told us that she knew the unofficial president of the Bandas, Des Alwi, and that he had guaranteed she would fly to Banda Neira that day, so we stayed close to her. Sure enough, we boarded the flight and reached the island, where a large sign, "Welcome Hockey," greeted us. Sadru had arranged for us to be met and taken to a hotel.

The huge, perfectly conical volcano of Gunung Api with its ever-present wisp of smoke shadows the island of Banda Neira. Eruptions of Gunung Api have caused the evacuation of the surrounding islands on many occasions, and evidence of recent larva flows can be seen running down to the sea. We chartered a boat to see the volcanic island from even closer, taking our snorkels and masks to check out the "new coral" at the underwater base of the volcano. It was an amazing view of stunning new growth and colours with myriads of tropical fish around the multitudinous shapes of the new coral. As we swam closer to shore from our boat, the water became even warmer than the standard tropical temperature until we were almost burned by the heat of the underwater hot springs. It was also enervating to swim in such warm water.

Back at the boat, our friend Vana, who had taken her own boat charter, met us. She was staying in Des Alwi's up-market hotel and she invited us to join her for cocktails that evening. Vana entertained us in style, compared to the usual modest accommodations we were used to. She told us of her life in Jakarta with her husband, Al, who worked under contract with the Indonesian Government, advising on environmental issues related to mining. When Vana learned that we would be returning to Vancouver through Jakarta in three months time, she insisted that we break our journey and let her show us Jakarta from an expatriot American's viewpoint.

Sadru and Farida had checked out the island thoroughly before we arrived so they knew exactly what we should do and see. They had not yet visited all the other islands in the Banda group so we took a local ferry to the island of Ai. We arrived just as a huge war canoe was being launched with the aid of a hundred strong men. The island of Ai was to compete in the Kora Kora races between Banda Neira and Gunung Api a week later. These races draw forty-man war canoes from all the neighbouring islands twice a year. We were lucky to be on hand to watch this spectacular battle of strength in front of our hotel. On Ai, we witnessed the blessing of the canoe, then found a perfect, empty beach where we got one of the natives to catch and cook some fish for us. While they cooked, we swam and snorkelled in the blue Banda Sea then relaxed under the swaying palms at the water's edge. We looked over to the next island, Run, and wondered who got the best deal when the British traded the island of Run to the Dutch in exchange for Manhattan in 1667.

The Spice Islands, and the Bandas in particular, were highly prized by the Portuguese, Spanish, Dutch and British who all fought over them at one time or another. The spices at stake were nutmeg, with its mace interior, cinnamon and cloves. We toured one of the few plantations on Banda Neira and viewed the various spices growing and being prepared for export. Mace and nutmeg from here is considered to be the best in the world and, perhaps, is one of the secret ingredients of Coca-Cola.

The next island to see was "Pisang" or Banana Island. We persuaded a boatman to take us there and to promise to return in two days and pick us up. On the way, we were sailing between some smaller islands when the skipper called out "lumpa, lumpa." Coming towards us was a school of dolphins, which completely surrounded our boat. It was a very moving experience to be so close to so many of these beautiful creatures in the wild.

We were the only guests on the island and the only guesthouse was right on the main beach with no other buildings in sight. There was a village of about a hundred people at the centre of the island and this was reached by a rough trail from the beach. There were no vehicles on the island, not even a wheel, and no electricity, either. It was primitive living yet we ate like kings on a diet of fresh fish, vegetables and fruit. The only thing missing was cold beer. The supply we had taken with us was consumed within the first few hours.

Snorkelling off the beach in front of our hut was the best we have seen anywhere in the world. There were hundreds of thousands of fish of all shapes, sizes and colours. On the opposite side of the island, about two hundred metres away, the shallows near the beach dropped off sharply fifty metres out. We snorkelled out over the underwater cliff and immediately encountered a two hundred kilogram cow fish. There was an abundance of all kinds of fish, the size of many more than slightly intimidating to us.

The sunsets from our hut were truly memorable. The sky turned a remarkable red as the sun sank behind the active Gunung Api volcano with its smoke curling upward. We could have stayed on Pisang for a week and done nothing but relax and enjoy the environment of this desert island.

Reluctantly, we returned to the main island of Banda Neira and said goodbye to Sadru and Farida who had their flight booked home to Vancouver. We tried to arrange to fly on to the Kei Islands but this proved impossible to do for weeks, so we booked onto a large ferry, which plied between the islands. It was not due to arrive for a few days, so we took the opportunity to further explore Banda Neira and some of the other islands. It was easy and inexpensive to arrange transportation by boat. At the island of Hatta, we were dropped into the water with our snorkelling equipment and a strong current swept us along a beautiful reef for miles before the escort boat picked us up. Noreen saw a shark but it wasn't interested in her as it had all the fish it could eat around him. We spent many hours on beaches and on shore, exploring museums and old forts.

Kei Islands and Pearls

The ferry arrived from Ambon loaded with thousands of visitors who were coming for the Kora Kora races. I have never seen so many people on a ship. It was still heavily overloaded when we left but we had elected to sail in first class. We had a good cabin on the top deck, so we were pretty comfortable. The trip to the Kei Islands took about eight hours and the sea was calm as we sailed through the night.

By this time, we had almost run out of money, as our stay in the Bandas had been longer than expected. There was no bank to exchange money or obtain a credit card advance in Banda Neira and the banks in Kei Kecil would not do so. Even the national airline office in Kei Kecil would not accept credit cards. We had some American dollars and eventually I found a Chinese merchant who gave me a supply of rupiah.

Meanwhile, Noreen was in a restaurant, guarding our luggage and being stared at by some of the local men, who found her somewhat of a curiosity. Some even sat at her table to get a better look at her. It was quite disturbing for Noreen and she was pleased when I returned to rescue her. We linked up with the only other travellers on the island, which included the German couple, Dietmar and Susan, whom we had met in Saparua.

The first project was to book our flights off the island of Kei Besar and we took a taxi to the airline office. While we were inside, Noreen was again left to guard the luggage. She again had to eject a man who clambered into the taxi with her.

Our group numbered eight, and we found some guest bungalows, without electricity, on one of the most perfect beaches in the world. The sand was a fine white powder, the sea was turquoise and palm trees leaned gently over the sand to provide shade from the sun in a blue sky with just the odd scattered clouds. There was no room for everyone at the bungalows but the village headman kindly gave up his bed in the village for Noreen and I.

One night there was enough though and we moved back to a vacated hut on the beach. One of the travellers then walked along the beach and found another group of new huts in the neighbouring village. There had been a road between the villages but it had been abandoned many years earlier after a dispute between the villages. Apparently, one village had helped the other build a church but the favour had not been returned, so a cold war had been proclaimed. The new huts had been completed months earlier but there was no sign so consequently they had never received any visitors. There was no electricity but still we decided to move and become their first guests. The owner was anxious to please us and even asked us how much he should charge us! The food was good but consisted of fish, fish and more fish.

The Kei Islands are known for their pearls so the group decided to take a boat to a pearl farm on an islet nearby. This island had never received any foreign visitors before so the locals were unsure if they should let us ashore. At that moment, there was a terrific thunderstorm so they invited us to take shelter in a small building. A French lady in our group was a gifted linguist who spoke eight languages. She was able to converse with the islanders who asked her where our guns were. The only exposure these people had to westerners was through the medium of television. They thought that we all carried firearms.

The operation was owned by Japanese interests but operated by Indonesians who were reluctant to divulge the secrets of pearl harvesting. In the end, they relented a little and showed us how the oysters were seeded and checked. When the rain finished, we sailed back to our huts in the open boat.

Our friends were all leaving before us so we spent our last night talking and dreaming of cold beer, joking that it had been promised along with chicken for days now. We were sad to say farewell to Emily from Seattle who taught river rafting and to Toph, a guy from England. We promised to meet up again with Dietmar and Susan from Germany and we shall one day soon. Noreen and I were alone on the beach for a couple of days and on our last night, the owner of the cottages finally produced a chicken for dinner. Our final wish was also granted when a motorcycle arrived from town carrying cold beer.

The next day, we took a bus back into town and attempted to fly back to Ambon. As usual, flights were unreliable, and we didn't fly until the following day. We flew back over the Banda Islands, which are like jewels in the gorgeous Banda Sea. Back in Ambon, we ran into Toph who was waiting for flights back to England. We also bumped into people we had met on the ferry to Saparua--and once again I couldn't help thinking *What a small world!*

Our plane from Ambon took us back through Sulawesi to Bali, where we stayed in our favourite hotels in Kuta and Candidasa. It was a shock to us, when we arrived in Bali, to find everything so civilized. There were proper bathrooms and toilets and even electricity. This is ironic as we suffer culture shock when we arrive in Bali from North America. The tourists we met in Candidasa were a very compatible group and there was instant bonding between people from Holland, France, Australia and Tasmania.

I mention Tasmania, in particular, as the people there are a little different from the mainland Australians. The Tasmanians we met were Floyd and Caroline, and they persuaded us to add "Tassie" to our itinerary. We did visit them in Launceston, Tasmania, and they showed us some of their wonderful island. The group in

Candidasa spent a lot of time together and we spent one
very happy evening celebrating the birthday of Philippe,
a Frenchman. It was a sad day when the group parted
ways and returned home, but we had more adventures
ahead of us in Australia and New Zealand.

Borneo, Island in the Clouds

One year after taking a group to Bali, we went to the
states of Sarawak and Sabah in Malaysian Borneo and to
Brunei. The decision to visit Borneo was an easy one, as
Malaysian Airlines offered us four stops on our journey
home without an extra charge. We decided to stop in
Kuching and Mulu in Sarawak, Kota Kinabalu in Sabah,
and Tokyo in Japan. It was an easy matter to take side
trips by air to Miri and Sandakan to see other parts of
Borneo.

The start of our trip in the new airport in Kuala
Lumpur was an event in itself. We had an early flight and
arrived before 5:00 A.M. to find the airport departure hall
busy, but no one was allowed past the security gate
except us. We found ourselves alone in the huge brand
new, high tech airport; it was quite an eerie feeling.
When the other passengers were allowed into the gate
area, we were the only foreigners. They were mostly
businessmen but there was also a local politician who
was a descendant of the head-hunters--complete with
extended ear lobes!

Kuching was our first destination and we checked
into the Holiday Inn. The hotels in Borneo were all
offering extremely low rates to try to encourage more
tourism, so we took advantage of this and stayed in some

very nice hotels. One of the things to do in Borneo is to visit a long-house. This is the typical home of a large family group of the Iban tribe, who are the original head-hunters. We arranged this with a local tour company and set off for the long bus ride to the Skrang River, followed by a pretty boat ride through the jungle.

They are quite used to receiving tourists in some longhouses, and it tends to be a commercial operation, that takes over the lives of the inhabitants. We were shown typical weaving and carving as well as the drying of pepper and other spices and foods. The headman gave a dance demonstration and showed us how to use a blow-gun. It was a long and expensive day out but very interesting, nevertheless. In future trips we are going to find a more authentic longhouse to visit. Preferably one that can be reached with less driving through monotonous jungle and more sailing up beautiful rivers.

We took our next trip without a guide. It was to Bako National Park and we used the local buses and longboats to reach our destination. Bako is situated on the shoreline and we were dropped on a very flat beach at low tide. The walk along the beach took us past unusual sandstone cliffs to the park office where maps were available. We chose a circular trek with a couple of spurs and set off into the jungle.

It was so hot and humid that we were pleased we had taken lots of drinking water. It was like walking through a sauna and we both lost pounds. The undergrowth was dense but a wooden walkway was provided to protect us from the creatures and beasts of the forest and to protect the forest floor. We spotted macaques and silver-leaf monkeys, wild boar and monitor lizards. Butterflies were in abundance and we watched hundreds of huge leaf-cutter ants carrying their outsized loads and making wide tracks on the jungle floor. The flora included orchids and a wide variety of tropical plants and trees. We spent only four hours on the trails but we could have spent a couple of days exploring the park.

When we returned to the park office, we were surrounded by scores of macaques that were quite aggressive, which was a little unnerving. Tourists often feed them and when there are only a few tourists, as there were that day, they demand to be fed. We enjoyed a wonderful cold drink after our sauna in the jungle, before we headed out onto the beach to catch our boat back to the bus for Kuching.

The following day, we again went into the jungle, this time to Gunung Gading National Park to look for the Rafflesia flower. These flowers are the largest in the world and can reach a metre in diameter. We had checked with the park office and had been advised that two flowers were in bloom. This was lucky as the blooms are rare and only last for four days before withering. We drove by local bus to the village of Lundu and took what we thought was a taxi to the park. It turned out that the "taxi" was actually the local police car. The police-chief driver would not accept a fare. A guide took us to see the Rafflesia flowers and they were magnificent. Their smell attracts insects, which get trapped in the flower with a sticky substance, which then dissolves and absorbs them. I took some beautiful photos and videos of the flowers.

The return buses are infrequent so we hitchhiked back to Kuching with a cellular telephone company vehicle. They were checking out coverage of the cellular system and they took us to some interesting remote villages on the convoluted drive back to town.

Borneo is pretty well organized with excellent roads and communications. Internet cafes are everywhere and the price for connection is small compared with North America and Europe. We e-mailed some of our friends, who were a little concerned about us being in the wilds of Borneo, and assured them that it was a very civilized area. The next stop on our journey was Miri, a short hop from Kuching and still in the state of Sarawak. We again checked in to the Holiday Inn and made our plans to visit Mulu and Brunei.

The kingdom of Brunei is just a few hours drive north of Miri and a tour operator, who wanted us to bring "Hot Tours" to Brunei, took us there. We were mainly ignored by the people of Brunei, 70 percent of whom are employed by the government. At the main mosque, we had to hand in our cameras before entering, and Noreen had to don a black robe, which covered her from head to foot. The mosque was a demonstration of extreme extravagance with its gilt, crystal chandeliers and Italian marble. Water taxis tear around the waterways within the city and we saw much of the city on stilts until we ran out of fuel. The waterways are quite polluted with garbage but the mosque areas are immaculately clean and tidy. After only a few hours, which we felt was enough, we returned to Miri via a company oil town, which boasted a huge monument commemorating the billionth barrel of oil pumped from the area.

Mulu is a resort village with its own airstrip, east of Miri. We went there in a small plane, which flew low over the jungle, and between limestone mountains, and landed on a dirt runway. The Royal Mulu Resort was really lovely and we were the only guests there. We arranged to take a hike into one of the many caves in the area. The first cave was the Deer Cave, the largest cave passage known to man. It could house St. Paul's Cathedral five times over. It is home to literally millions of bats and swiftlets. The swiftlets stay in the cave at night and forage for insects by day, while the bats forage by night. There were piles of excrement in the cave and the smell of ammonia was awful! It is estimated that about thirty tons are deposited daily. We watched in amazement and awe as wave upon wave of bats exited the cave at 5:00 P.M. Hundreds of thousands of bats were in each wave, covering the darkening sky and making a loud whirring as they passed over our heads.

After the half-hour show, we hiked back along the wooden walkway through the jungle, listening to the noises of the nocturnal creatures awakening. There were more caves to visit and this time we went upriver in a longboat, stopping at a native village on the way to buy woven and carved souvenirs. The Wind Cave, known for the constant cool breeze flowing through it and Clearwater Cave, the longest cave system in South-East Asia, are both most impressive. We returned to the Royal Mulu Resort for a comfortable night, and the following day we flew back to Miri and checked in to the sister hotel, the Rhiga Royal Hotel. It too was super-comfortable and we plan to take our group tours there.

We flew north, over Brunei to the state of Sabah and landed in the city of Kota Kinabalu. Sabah was formerly owned by the British North Borneo Company and the city of Kota Kinabalu was totally destroyed during World War II. Modern hotels are springing up at a faster rate than the tourists are coming, so good deals are easy to find. We wanted to check out several hotels for our future trips with groups, and we stayed in three fine establishments. We made contact with Rafflesia Tours, a local tour company run by Joseph, an Indian Malaysian. He really wanted our business and took us everywhere in his car. Joseph introduced me to the Marketing Manager of the brand new Pan Pacific Hotel, who happened to be a fellow Welshman and immediately we got on famously. He invited us to move into his hotel as his guest for a few days and we readily accepted. The Pan Pacific Hotel at Sutera Harbour was a luxury hotel and part of a complex that includes another large hotel, a marina and a golf course. It is on the ocean and commands fabulous views towards the offshore islands, which enhance the nightly sunset displays.

Joseph took us to a local Indian restaurant where we were served curry on a banana leaf accompanied by all kinds of exotic condiments. There was no beer in the restaurant but someone kindly ran up the road and brought back two huge cold ones for us.

Once a year, there is a grand market in a town called Kota Belud, a few hours drive north of Kota Kinabalu. We were lucky to be there at the right time so Joseph drove us there. We enjoyed shopping in the market and watching the local horsemen in their traditional costumes. There were no other tourists amongst the thousands of people in the market. We received many stares but also many smiles. I was invited to see a wedding ceremony and was ushered into a tent where the unhappy-looking bride was awaiting her fate. She was very young and her family had arranged her marriage. One old man put his arm around Noreen and insisted that I took his photograph.

Everything imaginable was for sale in the market from food to furniture. The only thing I bought was a wicked-looking knife with a razor-sharp blade. The handle was made of beautifully carved hardwood and the steel blade was also carved. It was a dangerous, yet useful, implement and is now a treasured souvenir.

We left Kota Belud for the mighty mountain, Mount Kinabalu, which stands at over four thousand metres. It became quite cool as we climbed, even though we were just six degrees north of the equator. The jungle turned into subtropical rainforest and there was a distinct change in the fauna and flora. A nature resort sits a short day's hike from the top and we stopped to check it out for future group tours.

The Sepilok Orang Utan Sanctuary is on the East Coast of Sabah. We reached it by flying from Kota Kinabalu to Sandakan and then by taxi to Sepilok. The Orang Utans or Wild Men of Borneo, in this reserve are in the process of being rehabilitated into the wild. Many are orphans of animals abandoned by their mothers, as forests and food sources become depleted. Others had been kept as pets until they became too large. Some grow to a hundred kilograms. In Sepilok, the Orang Utans are free to roam the forest but are fed a diet of bananas by the wardens. The limited diet is meant to encourage the animals to forage for themselves, as they soon become bored with bananas every day. Success of the rehabilitation program is judged by the Orangs mating with others in the wild. One success was noted by our guide, who pointed out a large mother called Noreen. She was carrying her baby whom we called Leah--after my Noreen's daughter.

The town of Sandakan was badly damaged during the war and is now a collection of rather uninteresting concrete buildings. Standing on a hill above the city there is a Chinese temple, from which is a panoramic view over Sandakan and towards the Philippine Islands not far off Borneo's coast. Unfortunately, we didn't have time to visit the nearby Turtle Islands to see turtles or the Kinabatangan River area to look for elephants. There is a herd of wild elephants, which we hope to find on our next trip to Sabah. The market in Sandakan mainly offers fish and products from the Philippines, but we also saw turtle eggs on display. When we went back to take photographs in the market, the illegally harvested eggs had been removed.

We returned to Kota Kinabalu and this time stayed downtown at the Hyatt Regency as their guests. The offshore islands form the Tunku Abdul Rahman Marine Park and are a short boat ride from the Hyatt. At the dock, men approached us and offered to take us over, but we decided to take the regular ferry-boat with the locals. We were most pleased that we did, as we were taken into the heart of a village built on stilts over the water. The ferry dropped us at a fancy resort on another island where we walked around the island on trails through the jungle and snorkelled from the sandy beaches. We were disappointed with the snorkelling, as fish dynamiting and recent hurricanes had destroyed much of the coral. When it was time to leave, we managed to hitch a ride on the staff boat and this took us on another tour of the islands of the Marine Park.

We took our leave of Sabah after a most interesting discovery tour, which was a real education for us. It has so much to offer and mostly in superlatives.

We loved all of Borneo and plan to return with a group in the near future. Hot Tours will continue to be a vehicle to carry us to faraway countries and cut down on our expenses for travelling, but it will never be a business. It will be a great way to travel and to make new friends all over the world, but it must *not* interfere with our retirement.

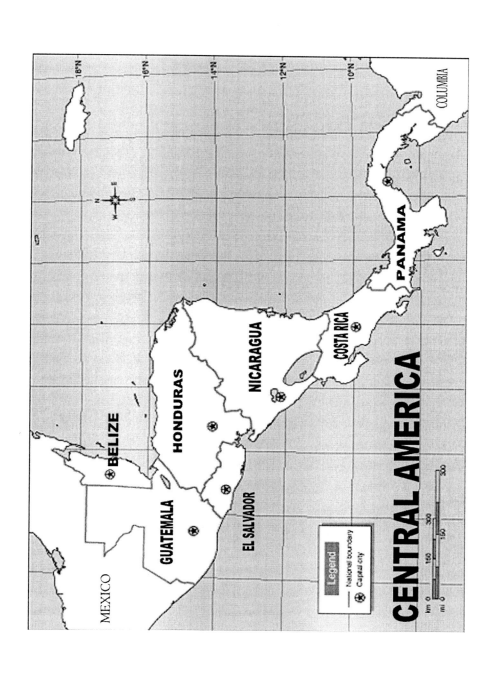

CENTRAL AMERICA

MEXICO

BELIZE

GUATEMALA

HONDURAS

EL SALVADOR

NICARAGUA

COSTA RICA

PANAMA

COLUMBIA

18°N
16°N
14°N
12°N
10°N

N
W   E
S

Legend
— National boundary
⊛ Capital city

km 0   150   300
mi 0   150   300

Nicaragua

Guanacaste

San Jose
*

Puerto Limon
*

Cahuita
*

*Londres

Quepos *
Manuel Antonio

Golfito

Osa

Panama

COSTA RICA

Pacific

Columbia

* Pasto

Ibarra

Ocean

Otavalo *

Quito *

ECUADOR

Banos

Guayaquil

Amazonia

Cuenca

Disputed Area

Peru

Chapter 5

Of Spaniards and Indios

Ecology is Synonymous with Costa Rica

Our first trip to Costa Rica was in 1989, almost a year before Noreen and I were married and only three months after we had encountered each other. We had met on a hike in the mountains near Vancouver and it had been a set-up. A lady I had seen a few times, who was also a good friend of Noreen, arranged it. Apparently, she had confided in Noreen that I was quite nice but too old for her, whereupon, Noreen had said, "Maybe he is not too old for me," and our mutual friend said she would arrange an introduction. It had taken about six months and finally the trap was laid: there would be a hike for Noreen to meet me, but I was to know nothing about the plan to introduce us.

The fatal day arrived and we had a major hike ending in an arduous downhill clamber, which stretched our leg muscles beyond the comfort level. The following day, I telephoned my friend to thank her for inviting me along and asked her how her legs were. She replied that they were a little sore and I then asked how Noreen's legs were. She suggested I ask her myself and gave me her phone number. The bait had been taken and I phoned Noreen to check on her legs and invited her out for dinner a week ahead. Our first date was a success and we started to see each other regularly.

For me, the difficult time of Christmas was coming and we decided to escape to parts unknown but warm. Our travel agent suggested Costa Rica and, thinking it was an island in the Caribbean, we said, "Book it." There were seats available on a charter flight but our agent could not find a hotel room for us. We told her to go ahead, anyway, and we would find accommodation after we arrived. Just before we were due to leave, we met a man who lived in Costa Rica who said he would meet us there and help us with accommodation.

We actually found a place from the *Lonely Planet* Guide Book and made a telephone booking. We then phoned our friend and left a message on his answering machine in San Jose, the capital of Costa Rica, telling him where we were staying. The day of our flight came and we were pretty excited about our first trip together and both were hoping it would go well.

By then we had discovered that Costa Rica was in Central America between Nicaragua and Panama, with coasts on the Pacific and the Atlantic Oceans. We landed at San Jose airport in the evening and followed the crowd of holidaymakers through the immigration process. We were then confronted with a large, computer generated sign, with the words "Mr. & Mrs. Newton Hockey."

Noreen looked at me suspiciously and wondered what I was up to. I was as much in the dark as she was, so we approached the man holding the sign and identified ourselves. He had been sent by our friend to meet us, expedite our entry (that is, bypass customs) and place us in a taxi complete with an armful of maps and information on Costa Rica. The taxi was in the VIP parking place at the exit of the airport and we were whisked off into the city. Our driver then told us that we were going to a different hotel from the one we had booked, as our friend wanted us to be in a better one. This set the stage for a memorable holiday where everything went well, though not according to plan, for we had none.

We only stayed in San Jose for a few days but quickly visited the tourist sights including the museum, art gallery and main square, and we immersed ourselves in our first Latin American country. Costa Rica is poor by North American standards but has a refreshing attitude towards life. Even in the city, people were outwardly friendly and greeted us with an "Hola" or "Buenos Dias." We felt that there was a large middle class and relatively small, poor and rich classes. This was reinforced when we travelled throughout the country. We learned that Costa Rica has no standing army and the money it saves goes towards education and health care. This makes a lot of sense to us.

The first excursion we made was on the Jungle Train to the east coast of the country. The train moved slowly through the suburbs of the capital and into the productive farmlands around San Jose in the Central Valley. It then entered the mountains and jungles, crossing many bridges and winding its way alongside rivers and cliffs covered in trailing vines and ferns interspersed with exotic flowers surrounded by colourful butterflies. We travelled second class with the locals and immediately made friends with our fellow travellers. Entrepreneurs brought all manner of food and drinks around the train. At each stop, a new band of vendors would get on to sell their wares. Although our Spanish was non-existent, somehow we managed to communicate with those around us, and they made us feel honoured and special.

Someone had advised us to finish the last leg of our trip to the coast by bus so that we could complete the journey in daylight. We alighted at Sigueres and looked around for the bus. In a moment, a large older black man approached us and somehow knew what we were looking for and beckoned us to follow him. Sure enough, we reached the bus station, and he indicated the office where we bought our tickets. While we were waiting, he stood near the bus, holding our place. This gratuitous gesture from a stranger was typical of many we experienced in Costa Rica and, later on, in other parts of Central America.

We reached Limon, a port town, with a predominately black population and took a taxi to our resort hotel just north of town. We heard that the black Caribbean people had until recent years been unable to travel more than ten miles from the coast. This has now all changed, I am pleased to say, and Blacks and Hispanics live side by side in harmony. Limon is quite dirty and rundown but the people are all very friendly.

The first evening we had dinner in a restaurant on stilts over the water. We would not be able to do this in later years, as shortly after we left Costa Rica there was a major earthquake. The quake lifted the shoreline, putting the restaurant well back from the sea. The earthquake also put an end to the Jungle Train, I am sad to say, but we feel fortunate to have made the trip before its ignominious end.

We took a long taxi ride south, down the coast, past pristine white sandy beaches, to the national park of Cahuita. There the palm trees and jungle come to the edge of the sand, making a picture-perfect beach scene, and we had it all to ourselves. We spent the whole day lazing around and swimming in the blue waters and trekking into the jungle to cool off and observe the fauna and flora of the area. The taxi driver waited all day to drive us back.

When it came time to leave Limon, we went to the bus station to book our tickets and were told that we would not be able to get on a bus until the following day, as it was just before Christmas and all seats were booked. This was a problem because we had arranged a ride from San Jose to the West Coast at noon that day. We contacted our hotel by phone and they said they would find a taxi which would take us; it was up to us to go to the market-place where the taxi driver would find us. This sounded like an expensive option and how would the taxi find us? About half an hour later, we were walking near the market and the taxi appeared, somehow recognizing us, and took us to pick up our luggage before heading to San Jose. He told us the fare would be $25, more expensive than the bus but still a bargain for crossing half the country.

The trip started badly with the taxi driver careening like a madman. We had told him we were in a hurry to rendezvous with a friend and he was determined to be early. A flat tire stopped us for ten minutes and he then drove even faster to make up for lost time. The road was all paved but there were numerous hills and blind corners, and the driver assumed there were no other vehicles on the road coming towards him and overtook anywhere. We tried to appreciate the spectacular mountain and jungle scenery but it was difficult from the speeding taxi.

We made our rendezvous in San Jose with time to spare and met an American in a pick-up truck who was to take us to Puntarenas on the west coast. First we went to a hotel for refreshments and there met a family with four children. They had just picked up two orphans from an orphanage and were taking them back to the United States to join two others they had adopted earlier. We admired their generosity and dedication.

Puntarenas is a port city and a bit of a dump, but we had to stay there in order to catch a ferry to the Nicoya Peninsula the following day. We had met a Canadian in Vancouver, who had a hotel in Bahia Gigante, on the peninsula, and we planned to spend Christmas there--we had even paid a deposit.

When we arrived at the ferry dock on the peninsula, it was getting dark and we went to a restaurant to phone the hotel for transportation as we had been instructed. Unfortunately, the telephone lines were down from a recent storm and there was no way to contact the hotel. There were no taxis or buses and no one could take us there. We sat and thought over a beer or two (Had we been scammed? Had we lost our deposit?). Our only option seemed to be to sleep in the restaurant, as there was no accommodation available. We were resigned to this when out of the dark appeared a truck and a man came in and said he had come to take us to Bahia Gigante. We still don't know how he came but we were definitely grateful. Apparently, the hotel owner had our arrival date wrong.

The hotel was new and comfortable but the local pigs had not been trained to keep clear of the swimming pool and grounds, making walking around a trifle messy. The local beach was nothing to write home about so we rented horses and went exploring and found beautiful, deserted bays not far away. On Christmas Day we found a piece of paradise and tied our horses under a tree, set to spend the day on the beach. Our peace was shattered when two other people appeared. This was no problem. We just jumped on the horses and found another deserted beach and swam all day in the clear waters of the Gulf of Nicoya--along with some stingrays.

On Boxing Day we were invited for a day's outing with a couple who were sailing around the world in a forty-foot sailboat. We sailed around some offshore islands and swam from the boat off a long sandy beach while our host baked cookies in the galley. The gorgeous sunset was a fitting conclusion to a perfect Christmas.

To go to the south of Costa Rica, we had to retrace our route on the ferry and take a bus. We arrived in the National Park of Manuel Antonio and found that all the hotels were full for the New Year holiday. This is what our travel agent had warned us about. We phoned our friend in San Jose and he soon fixed us up in a hotel, which was still under construction. It was pretty rough and when we returned to our room after dinner, a frog greeted us as it jumped past our faces. A large family of cockroaches, which must have had a prior booking and hadn't checked out, also greeted us. The following day we moved into a brand new unit and the rest of our stay in Manuel Antonio was fabulous.

The area is popular with tourists, as the beaches are endless. At holiday times, the Costa Ricans join the tourists for party time with music and dancing. Finally, it was time to head home, and we hitched a ride with a French Canadian who insisted on checking out every place that sold beer between Manuel Antonio and San Jose. Fortunately he wasn't driving but we realized why he drank when we saw the tortuous, rough, unpaved mountain road with hairpin bends and sheer drops on alternate sides.

We spent one more night, New Years Eve, in San Jose and were disappointed not to find a party, but most of the locals were still at the coast. The last night we spent in the mountains above the city at the hotel where our friend was the cook. The food was wonderful and the view spectacular. We finished our holiday on a high point. Noreen and I had survived two weeks together in all kinds of situations and there was certainly some stress at times. We didn't have any disagreements however. Maybe this relationship would work.

The next time we visited Cost Rica we did so as a married couple and planned to stay several months in one place to get a proper feel for the country and its people. We chose the Manuel Antonio/Quepos area as we had enjoyed that the most on our first trip. We found an apartment, which we rented on a monthly basis for a very reasonable rate, on a hill with sweeping views over the coastline. We were on the top floor of the apartment and at the same level as the treetops. This gave us a perfect vantage point to observe toucans and other exotic birds and parrots at eye level.

We would walk down to the beach almost every day through jungle, which was home to troupes of white face and spider monkeys. I started to read lots of books, a luxury I had denied myself for years. Sure, I knew how to read, but all the reading material had been technical books, magazines and newspapers.

It is easy to meet people who are on holiday, as they are relaxed and friendly. In this way, we made many superficial friends. We also began to meet the locals who recognized that we were staying longer than most other visitors were. We were invited to parties and met even more expatriates and locals.

One party was in a village called Londres, some ten miles inland in farmland at the base of the mountain range that divides the country from north to south. This gave us a totally new perspective on the country--we saw the agricultural side where crops of citrus fruits, bananas, pineapple and spices were grown. We saw groves of Mango trees loaded with fruit, most of which dropped to earth for the cattle to eat--what a waste of delicious fruit! We became friends with an American farmer who had horses but no time to ride them. He was only too pleased to have us exercise them for him. We found some terrific trails into the jungle and along riverbeds where there were scores of butterflies, some an electric blue with enormous wingspans. We were miles from civilization, just the two of us in the jungles of Central America--and no one knew where we were.

Londres is a sleepy little village where everyone knows everyone else and all strangers are immediately identified. We spent a fair bit of time there and came to know many of the inhabitants. Two friends had vanilla plantations and we hadn't realized that vanilla is a kind of parasite that lives on host trees, rather like orchids. The vanilla beans are picked and then set in alcohol to make the vanilla extract. We tried it ourselves, let some beans sit in vodka for a year and we now have several years supply of extract. We picked pepper, boiled it in water for half an hour and dried the peppercorns in the sun for a few days to give us hard black corns to take home. We also picked red chilli peppers and dried them to take home. There is something about the fruits of one's own labour that makes them taste extra special.

Horse Riding in the Jungle

The most memorable horse ride was when we were invited to join a group of Costa Ricans on an expedition to find some caves in the mountains of Cerro Muerte. There were nine riders with two packhorses. Two of the riders were campesinos acting as guides. The organizer was a gentleman farmer called Vinicio, who operated a bus importing business in San Jose. He would drive old school buses from the U.S.A. to his factory and rebuild them for the terrible roads of Costa Rica. His beautiful girlfriend, Alejandra, accompanied him on the trek. Also with us was an American, Rick, and his athletic wife, Ileana, who was a gold medallist cyclist in the Pan American Games. Rick had moved from Alaska where he ran a windshield repair shop and had opened a similar shop in San Jose. About the only thing that Alaska and Costa Rica have in common is bad roads.

We set off at 4:30 A.M. in total darkness and began to climb very steeply almost immediately. We passed peasants headed down the mountain on foot with goods for the market. It was hot going, even at that time of the morning. We stopped only briefly from time to time for drinks and by noon we had reached a campesino's hut with an outstanding view over idyllic scenery of cleared land and jungle. We understood the reason for the early start when the heavens opened just after we arrived and the downpour lasted several hours while we rested after our long trek.

In the evening we cooked the chilli con carne that we had prepared at home and frozen for the journey and sang songs on the deck to the strains of a guitar played by Ileana. Other than our oil lamp and candles, there were no lights for miles, and the stars shone more brightly than we had ever seen before. We went to bed early that night to prepare for our trek on horseback and on foot the following day.

The going was steep and tough, and finally we had to abandon the horses and slash our way through the jungle with machetes. We came across a valley, which had been cleared for crops, and a farmhouse near a river. One of our guides approached the farmhouse, spoke with the farmer's wife and told us he had arranged for lunch for our group on our return from the caves.

The final assault to the caves involved an arduous climb, which was made worse by the heat of the midday sun, but we all made it and entered the cool caves with relief. The only light we had was from our flashlights, and it was pretty eerie, especially when we realized that few people had ever been here before us. The local residents of the cave were enormous spiders, and we soon cooled off and left for the safety of the daylight outside. The clamber down to the farm was quite tricky but the thought of food and a cool drink drove us on. We were somewhat dehydrated and drank voraciously from a nearby stream.

The farmhouse with its mud floor kitchen was a surprise to us, but it also boasted a sleeping area of beautiful wood floors in a series of bunk- bedded rooms, all in immaculate shape. The lady had borne twenty-two children and twenty-one were alive with most still living at home. A new grandchild, less than a week old, was being nursed, and other grandchildren were scattered around the house and garden. A grand feast had been prepared for us--after all, what are nine more guests for lunch?

After lunch we relaxed and enjoyed the outstanding jungle scenery and watched as twelve toucans flew into a tree nearby. I was able to catch this rare sight on my video camera. We returned to pick up our horses and make our way back to our campesino's house for another night, totally exhausted. Our guides were not tired and they unsaddled and washed the horses down for us.

The guides were up before us in the morning and had saddled all the horses and loaded the packs ready for our trek home to Londres. We reached the ranch from where we had started and felt tired but happy after the unique experience our new Tico (Costa Rican) friends had given us. The whole trip was free to us and the guides refused any payment. We got around this, though, by giving them some tools, which they could use in their fields. We were able to relive our trip a week later by looking at my video in San Jose; in fact, we have done so on several occasions in Canada as well. I shall always remember the woman with twenty-two children and the twelve toucans in one tree outside her house.

A visitor's visa in Costa Rica is only valid for three months and then it is necessary to leave the country for seventy-two hours before re-entering for another three months. Some people fly to San Andreas Island, part of Columbia, not far from the Costa Rica East Coast. Others drive north to Nicaragua or south to Panama. We chose to drive to Panama with two friends, one Tica and one American, George. At the border town, we parked our rental car and walked to the immigration office to have our passports stamped with an exit stamp and proceeded to Panama to be stamped-in to that country. Now we were legally in Panama but entered the back door of a shop and left by the front door, which opened into Costa Rica. We were now in Costa Rica illegally, of course, and we walked back to our car to drive back to Golfito, a port town opposite the Osa Peninsula.

We had hardly driven a mile when we were stopped by the police and asked for our papers. They would have shown that we were in Panama so we had to say our papers were back in our hotel in Quepos, a day's drive north. The policeman seemed to buy our story but asked to look in the trunk of the car, which he did but didn't spot anything out of order. He stepped back, I saluted him and thanked him for his courtesy, and he allowed us to proceed.

We went on to the dutyfree zone in Golfito where we stocked up on duty free goods and stayed two nights before reversing our border crossing procedure and coming back into Costa Rica legally for another three months. This is one of several ways in which people get around the silly regulations that some Central American countries make. At least in Honduras one can get a visa renewed at a local immigration office without leaving the

country but there they want you to do it every month.
The added complication about Honduran regulations is
that you have to buy a special stamp, only available at a
particular bank, before taking it to immigration. Another
illogical thing is that, if you drive in your own vehicle,
the visa for you is valid for one month and that for the car
is valid for three months. To renew the car visa you have
to go to the capital and get a certain man to give you
special permission. No other person can do this very
important job. I shall have more to say about such "catch-
22" regulations in my chapter on Honduras.

A big problem for expatriates in Costa Rica and in
many other tropical retirement zones is that they have
nothing to do. As a result, they resort to drinking alcohol,
which is generally quite cheap, at least for the locally
distilled hooch. This often means the drinking starts in
the morning and by noon many are well in the bag. Our
special friend, George, had an enormous capacity for
booze and could always be seen with a glass in his hand
any time after five in the afternoon. He is a very
generous and compassionate man and oneday when he
learned that a friend of his had lost her mother, he
whisked the friend, Noreen and me off to a village out of
town to entertain and distract her from her loss. George
took us to a bar where there was a Ping-Pong table and a
jukebox and proceeded to ply us with drinks of beer and
guarro (the local hooch). Soon none of us were feeling
any pain; I was playing Ping-Pong with the five-year-old
daughter of our bereaved friend on my shoulders. Noreen
was commiserating with the others over songs played on
the jukebox, sharing the loss of their respective mothers.

Somehow we drove back to Quepos in an
inebriated state and I resolved never to drink guarro

again. Unfortunately a year later, alcoholism caught up with our friend, George, and he suffered a stroke which has left him partially paralysed and with difficulty in speaking and handling numbers. Even this, though, did not stop him drinking and he has had another stroke and continues to drink. Such is the nature of alcoholism. We still hear from George from time to time and reminisce over the good times we had with him in Costa Rica. He used to take us to all the parties in town in his beaten-up Volkswagen jeep, carrying his large container of booze. We lived with him for a few months and marvelled at his stamina with the scores of girlfriends he brought home. At night, he would fall asleep watching videos of *Fawlty Towers* episodes. He never did see the endings.

Columbia

On one of our trips to Costa Rica, we decided to head further south and visit Ecuador. The travel agent suggested that the cheapest way was first to fly north-west to the island of San Andreas, Columbia, and take a domestic flight to Columbia. From there we could go overland to Ecuador. If we were to do that, it would make sense to actually see a little of Columbia on the way, so we planned to stay overnight in San Andreas and check out the beaches.

We found that San Andreas is quite beautiful but also crowded. It is a duty-free island and there were throngs of people in and around the scores of electronics and perfume stores. At the airport, we had to go through a body and baggage search before entering the boarding lounge. We were held in the lounge for ages before our flight to Cali. We never did hear our flight called and I asked the agent about our expected departure time. He said we should get on the plane that was then boarding. The doors closed and the flight attendant announced we were going to Cartagena. We thought it was an intermediate stop and enjoyed our view of the city from the air.

We took off again but this time they announced we were going to Bogota, the capital. We were still not concerned, but when we reached Bogota, everyone was ordered off the plane, as that was the termination of the flight. The agent at the gate told us there were no more flights on to Cali and we would have to stay the night in a hotel at the airline's expense. We convinced the agent that we should take an afternoon flight the next day so that we could see a little of Bogota. A taxi was hired to do a city tour and we drove around for several hours.

The place I remember best was the palace, which was bristling with well-armed soldiers. I wanted to take a picture but the taxi driver was afraid to stop. I also remember seeing the Intercontinental Hotel where the Escobar family were under armed guard after recent drug battles and arrests. We found the city quite intimidating and not at all safe. The people appeared to be very serious.

Cali was a different story altogether. It was a Sunday when we checked into our simple hotel downtown. We knew that Cali was the centre of the drug cartel and was considered dangerous. The U.S. State Department had warned U.S. citizens to stay away from Columbia and especially from Cali. Undaunted, we strode out into the crowds in the central park area and found them to be families out for their Sunday stroll.

Smiles, waves and calls greeted us, and we felt secure and comfortable; the citizens were most welcoming. Cali is an attractive Spanish colonial city, slightly run-down but still busy and alive. We walked around the central areas, which were very relaxed on Sunday. By Monday morning it was a normal busy city, and the market was in full swing with goods brought in from surrounding villages by Hispanic and indigenous people.

Our journey towards Ecuador continued by local bus from Cali to Pasto, through spectacular mountain country, past huge coffee estates. More than one fenced compound was guarded by towers manned by private armies of the drug lords, armed to the teeth. Pasto was another colonial town and seemed quite depressed. The people were less friendly than those in Cali and often avoided looking at us. We only stayed one night and carried on to the Ecuador border.

On the Equator in Ecuador

My first impression of Ecuador was that it looked a little like England with rolling hillsides dotted with small fields and the occasional farmhouse. Llamas and donkeys were used to carry huge loads from the fields. The temperature was cool, for the elevation is high even though we were almost at the equator.

Our first stop was in Ibarra, and we checked into a hotel where we made it known that we were considering bringing groups to Ecuador. This gave us a good rate in the hotel and the manager insisted on giving us a tour of the surrounding countryside on the following day. He took us by car into beautiful countryside with colourful towns, villages and hamlets all inhabited by Indians. They were mostly coy about having their photographs taken as they feel that their spirit may be stolen from them. We respected their wish and only took photographs from a distance. There were those Indians who were not as sensitive but they would ask for money--and we don't pay for photographs. We therefore only have a few photos of these colourful people, but those we took are charming.

We visited Lake Yaguarcocha, meaning Lake of Blood, where 10,000 Indians were reportedly thrown after a battle, turning the waters red with blood. Our guide had a small Spanish school in Ibarra and tried to convince us to be his representative in Canada. There are several Spanish schools in the town and I imagine it would be a wonderful experience to learn the language in that temperate climate with beautiful surroundings and to live with an Ecuadorian family.

Just south of Ibarra is Otovalo, a small town with a big market. It is central to a large number of weaving villages. The indigenous people in their traditional, brightly coloured shawls and sombreros go there every day and set up their stalls in the main square. The markets on Wednesdays and Sundays are the busiest and they attract both wholesale and retail buyers from Quito and around the world. Cotton and woollen woven goods are the principal products and they are in the form of rolls of material and finished shawls, as well as rugs and wall hangings.

We wished to buy almost everything, but we knew we had to carry what we bought. And we still had to travel through the rest of Ecuador, back to Costa Rica and then home to Vancouver. We limited our purchases to some wall hangings, a poncho and two Panama hats. Leather products such as beautiful briefcases and ladies handbags, were also for sale. I bought a carved leather belt for three dollars and a large bag (to carry our purchases) for thirty dollars. The latter would have cost well over a hundred dollars at home.

One day we wandered out of town along country lanes, which were paved with neatly laid stones in intricate patterns. The stones had obviously been in place for many years and had probably been laid under the direction of the conquering Spaniards. They were still in excellent condition and led us to some charming villages. The villages were almost deserted in the midday sun, but from within the houses came the clattering sound of looms. Weaving was a real cottage industry. In another village they specialized in leather making; the expensive products they produced belied their place of manufacture. The price paid for one briefcase in Vancouver would pay a family for a month in one of these villages.

We carried on by bus to Quito, climbing slowly and sometimes not so slowly to ten thousand feet. Quito stands on the steep sides of several mountains, which form a dramatic backdrop for the picturesque city. We stayed in the smart area of the city near the embassies, fashionable hotels and residences, but in a budget place. It was a safe area and we walked around, even at night, exploring the interesting shops and restaurants. There were many foreigners in evidence doing the same thing. The old town is some distance away and we took a taxi through crowded winding streets to the square with the royal palace. Toy Guards, reminiscent of the toy soldiers in the *Nutcracker Suite* stood at attention in front of the palace.

We walked for miles around the principal streets and then I noticed a small group of young men following us. We finally stopped at a busy corner, stared at them for a while and eventually they moved off. We had been warned of attacks on foreigners and to keep to well-travelled areas. We heard of robberies on the trail up to the cross that dominates Quito so we took another taxi to this strategic lookout point. We marvelled at the extensive view in all directions, especially south towards the famous Andes.

We had planned to take the train to Guayaquil but heard some bad reports from fellow travellers. Instead, we rented a car and first headed for the Amazonia region, which is where the various tributaries of the mighty Amazon rise.

First we had to cross the Andes through a mountain pass at thirteen thousand feet. The car was breathless, as were we at that altitude. It was pretty lonely up there but we enjoyed the views of smooth rocks on the mountain peaks and the sight of eagles swooping around them. The road continued down the other side through remote villages where we were very conspicuous in our rental car. Most tourists to the area travel by local bus. At the end of the road into the steamy jungle, we parked our car in a secure hotel and spent a hot night trying to get some sleep.

Many people take a trip down the river for several days and stay in local villages. We felt we needed only an appreciation of the area. We did not need to subject ourselves to discomfort and the mercy of the mosquitoes and other creatures, so we asked around for ideas for a day trip. Somehow we found an Indian couple who were going to their village downstream and returning later the same day.

Noreen and I climbed into a small rocky dugout canoe with an even smaller motor and set off to explore the Amazon jungle. The ride was quite precarious, especially when we hit the shallows and rapids but, all in all, it was exciting, as we had no idea where we were going and nobody in the world knew where we were. We were taken along a narrow trail through high grass, sugar cane and forest and found ourselves in a small clearing where there was a wooden house on stilts. This was the home of our guides and where they farmed for bananas, corn, sugar and root crops. It was a very simple home and afforded little protection from the animals and insects of the jungle. I am glad we had decided not to rough it there. I was taught the ancient art of using a blowgun with a poison dart, but I would probably starve if it were my only way to catch food.

We returned to the boat with a pot of orange-coloured substance, headed further into the jungle, and were taken to another clearing where a root crop had been planted. Some roots were pulled and carted to the boat to be taken to market; it was tough work, I discovered, when I attempted to help. When we were back in the boat and were headed upstream, our host offered me a drink of orange-coloured liquid, which I accepted, as it would appear rude to refuse. I drank some, to the horror of Noreen who had seen how it was made. The thick brown substance from the house had been diluted with water from the river, the same muddy water used as a sewer and for bathing and laundry. Noreen took the cup and pretended to drink and was convinced that I would be sick while she escaped that fate. In fact I was fine and the "substance" had no effect on me. It would have been interesting to know what I had been drinking but we could not communicate that well with our guides. They had their own language and couldn't even speak Spanish. It was certainly a wonderful river trip, which we will long remember.

The next stop was in the town of Banos, which, as the name implies, is a bath town where hot springs feed swimming pools with murky brown, healing mineral water. We decided to take the plunge and test the waters with hundreds of other people but I did so with our hotel room key in my pocket. Naturally it fell into the opaque water and was lost. I mentioned this to the manager in case someone found it, and he took my loss very seriously. An announcement was made and the huge pool was emptied and, lo and behold, a small boy found our key and handed it to us!

Banos is a typical spa town with lots of hotels and restaurants busy with people "taking the waters." It is set in a scenic valley, half way between Amazonia and the Andes. We found it quite relaxing there, but we had to press on and make our way south to Cuenca. This is another typical colonial city with attractive architecture in the Spanish style. While we were in Cuenca, almost every street was dug to replace all the underground services. It did not occur to anyone to do the work in stages. The maximum disruption to traffic and business took place all at once, inconveniencing the whole population at the same time. In spite of the appearance of the streets and the gridlocked traffic, we liked Cuenca and hope to return someday. It was a friendly city but we couldn't find anyone who spoke English, so our meagre Spanish was forced to the surface. We understood more than we had thought we could and managed to communicate with people. This was as far south as we travelled in Ecuador and we had to start our return trip in order to catch our flight to Canada from San Jose, Costa Rica.

The drive north to Quito was on the main highway, which runs past a row of magnificent volcanoes that are part of the mighty Andes. We stayed another night in Quito and retraced our route by bus all the way back to Cali, Columbia, where we enjoyed another night. We flew back to the island of San Andreas where, again, we spent a day and a night. The security at the airport for our flight to Costa Rica was very high. After the initial bag and body search at the entrance by machine-gun toting guards, we waited in the holding lounge and watched the luggage being stacked near a plane on the apron. When our flight was called, we had to identify our bags and have them checked again by drug-sniffing dogs before they were loaded. All this was under the scrutiny of soldiers wielding AK 47's, which was quite intimidating. Once on the plane we started to relax until the dogs were brought on the aircraft to have another sniff. We were glad to get off the flight in San Jose and return to the relatively gun-free Costa Rica.

Costa Rican Bugs

We only had a few days before we had to go to Vancouver so we rushed around to say our good-byes to friends in different parts of the capital and the coast. One of my Tico friends, Vinicio, took me to a local pub where they served bocas (appetizers) with the beer. I tried some deep fried shrimp and they seemed delicious, but the following day I started to have stomach problems. My condition deteriorated rapidly and I was losing fluids from all apertures. A doctor was called and she prescribed some drugs and suggested I go home to Canada, as soon as possible, for further treatment. I was in no state to drive so Noreen had to take the wheel. She was, fortunately, named as an alternate driver for our rental car and had to drive me through the mountains on those treacherous roads back to San Jose for our flight home.

When we changed planes in Houston, I was so weak that I had to use a wheelchair and the same happened in Seattle. Noreen telephoned a friend in Vancouver and it was arranged for us to be picked up and driven directly to the emergency ward of the hospital. I was immediately put on intravenous fluids and antibiotics, and blood tests were carried out. The tests showed that I had two bacteria, camplerbacter and shigella, and the antibiotic I had taken in Costa Rica was only effective on one of them. Within twenty-four hours of taking a new prescription, I was feeling much better, though I was still very weak. In just five days I had lost fifteen pounds--a fast way to lose weight but not one that I would recommend.

The moral of the story is not to eat food in third world pubs unless you are sure they use western standards of hygiene. Vinicio had no ill effects as his body can handle the bugs.

Mexico

B
E
L
I
Z
E

Tikal
*

La Mesilla
Huehuetenango
*

Chichicastenango
*

Chiquimula
*
Honduras

Guatemala City
*

Panajachel*
Lake Atitlan

Antigua*

*Agua Calientes

El Salvador

GUATEMALA

Chapter 6

New Jungles, Beaches and Carpets

Honduras

Costa Rica is a lovely country and we enjoyed visiting it for four years until it became rather expensive for our retirement budget. We appreciated Central America's climate, oceans and jungles and we also liked it because it is not too far from Canada. We thought we should see a little of the other countries in the area, which were less developed than Costa Rica.

We flew to Mexico City and connected to a Taca flight to San Salvador in El Salvador. Our flight was late and we thought we would miss our connecting flight to San Pedro Sula in Honduras. We were hustled to our new gate where an aircraft was in the final boarding mode; the door closed as soon as we were seated. We groaned at the thought that our baggage would never be transferred in time and resigned ourselves to living in dirty clothes for a day or two. We need not have been concerned, though, as our bags were waiting for us in San Pedro Sula. The airport was little more than a shed and customs clearance was just a formality.

Soon we were at a taxi stand full of empty taxis and lots of people waiting. It transpired that the highway to town had been blocked by a workers' demonstration and no one knew when the road would be open. After an hour or two, traffic started to move and, after a slow drive, we reached the city centre and found a hotel.

We spent a day exploring the central area and looked for the train station. Our guidebook said there was a train running through the plantations of the United Fruit Company to Tela. We found the station but it was deserted and the rails were rusty; we were obviously going to have to find alternative transport so we chose the bus. Tela is a sleepy village on the north coast of Honduras. It was once an active company town for the shipment of fruit to North America, but the warehouses were now derelict and the company houses had been turned into a holiday resort. We stayed right down town where we could see a little action.

The first day it rained so much that all the streets were flooded under two feet of muddy water. The locals were used to this and ingeniously produced all kinds of planks and stepping stones in order to get around town without getting their feet wet. We visited the office of the local National Park and arranged to take a boat trip to Punta Sal, a park only accessible by water on a point of land about an hour away.

The next day, we walked down the beach to the mouth of a river where we found the boat we had hired. We were to share the boat with other travellers. One was a Honduran, Rod, who was an architect living in the States, but who wanted to return to Tela to build a resort.

Rod just loved being back in his home country, and when we arrived at the park he dived into the warm clear waters fully clothed. He did this because of his exuberance but we noticed later that it is a common custom to swim clothed, possibly because people cannot afford swim suits. Why bother to change, anyway, when clothes dry on your back in no time in the tropics?

Another passenger was Suzy, a freelance writer for the *New York Times* and the *Guardian* amongst other well-known newspapers. She was English but lived in Montreal. She was doing a story on the fate of "The Disappeared," people who had mysteriously vanished under previous governments, and was also covering the murder of a prominent local environmental activist, Jeanette Kawas. Punta Sal Park had been dedicated as a park, but people had been allowed to cut trees and Ms Kawas had tried to stop the loggers, making herself rather unpopular with some people, including a prominent military officer. Suzy was visiting the park for a first- hand look and to interview some of the local people who all knew the real story but were afraid to tell authorities who were themselves corrupt.

The park is really beautiful, with its sandy beaches, rocky outcrops, thick jungle and abundant fauna and flora. Rod was a little concerned about poisonous snakes, which are native to the area. He had been in South America one time and been bitten by a snake. His life had been saved by the prompt action of a local Indian who found a natural antidote growing nearby. Our guide assured Rod that he too knew the antidotes, but we were very careful to watch for snakes on the ground and hanging from trees. We traversed the point and were picked up on the opposite side of the peninsular by our boat and taken to a small collection of huts where local Garifuna people prepared a delicious meal of fish.

Our journalist friend, Suzy, conducted her interviews and I took some photographs for her. On our return to Tela, she asked me to take more photos, this time of the murder scene. She was actually staying in the room in which the murder had taken place, and I took photos of bullet holes in the window shades and of the chair where the victim had sat. It was pretty eerie, as nothing in the room had changed since the murder; all the victim's books were still on the shelves where she had left them. I mailed the developed photos and negatives to Suzy and promptly lost her address so I never found out if the story was published. I hope it was, and I hope our intrepid friend did not suffer the same fate as Jeanette Kawas. She enjoyed being in the face of danger, and she herself had been shot covering stories in El Salvador a few years earlier. The Punta Sal Park is now known as the Jeanette Kawas National Park.

Bicycles were available for rent in the town so we used them to visit some of the Garifuna villages nearby. The Garifunas are descendants of black African slaves who were released by the British on the Caribbean Island of St. Vincent over two hundred years ago. They had then migrated to the coasts of Guatemala, Honduras and Nicaragua. Many of them speak English as well as their own Garifuna language and the official language, Spanish. We met a hundred-year-old blind man who was pleased to tell us about the old times on the coast. Not much has changed in the last two hundred years and the Garifunas still live in tiny mud huts near the beach and fish for their livelihood.

The United Fruit Company established a botanical garden in the early part of the century. In it are many species of tropical trees and shrubs native to the Americas and Africa. They are well established, and although the gardens were neglected for years after the pullout of the Company, they have been re-established and are well worth a visit. They are called the Lancetilla Gardens and are located just west of the town of Tela.

We bussed along the coast eastwards to La Ceiba, the third largest town in Honduras after the capital, Tegucigalpa, and San Pedro Sula. La Ceiba was named after a large Ceiba tree that used to stand near the waterfront but has long since disappeared. The port facilities for the shipment of fruit are also long gone. All that remains are disused rail lines and old buildings. In spite of this, the town is active with secondary industries and commerce.

We continued on to Trujillo, which is at the eastern end of the paved road in the country. We immediately fell in love with the sleepy town of friendly people. Our home for two weeks was the Villa Brinkley, a hotel with a commanding view of the town and the whole sweep of Trujillo Bay with its miles of white sandy beaches. The hotel itself was a large rambling place with many levels and built in the Spanish style with tiled roofs and patterned concrete flagstones. All the doors and columns were made from beautiful carved hardwoods, which had taken one man ten years to make.

The venerable owner was Peggy Brinkley who had supervised the building of the hotel over a period of some twenty years. When she first started, there was only a horse trail to the site; now it is not much better but cars can make it with a struggle. The hotel has been in a state of construction since day one and nothing ever seems to be completed. There are always loose tiles on the roof, the pool is rarely working and when it is, the water is murky. It has a charm like that of Fawlty Towers and the restaurant food is consistently good. The ever-present Dona Peggy is an essential part of the hotel, but at over eighty years of age, she is slowly losing her touch and the hotel is deteriorating. Peggy Brinkley is an American and very much part of Trujillo. She has a most generous nature and has helped innumerable citizens and visitors to Trujillo all of whom treat her with the utmost respect.

Near Trujillo, Columbus first landed on the mainland of the Americas and, for a while, Trujillo was the capital of Honduras. Since then, its only claim to fame was when William Walker, the self-proclaimed American ruler of Nicaragua and Honduras, was captured by the British. He was handed over to the Hondurans who summarily executed him. Walker is buried in the old cemetery where a few travellers make the pilgrimage to see his headstone. Another stone in the hospital grounds marks the spot where he was shot.

Nothing much happens now in Trujillo, but anything that does happen is known instantly throughout the community. There is a local radio station and the ex-patriots have a marine band radio system that effectively tells everyone, everyone else's business. We became very attached to the town and the next chapter has much more to say about Trujillo.

During our first visit, the nightlife was very active, especially at weekends. The favourite places were: the Rincon de Los Amigos, a beach bar that featured live Garifuna music and dancing; two discotecs in town; and several places in Cristales, the Garifuna barrio attached to

Trujillo. Travellers stayed in the cheap budget hotels, including Albert's Place, a rambling old mansion that also housed a language school. More up-market tourists would stay at the Villa Brinkley, O'Glynn's or the Christopher Columbus. The latter was known locally as the Big Green Laundry due to its brightly coloured exterior and its alleged connection with drug-carrying planes, which could land on the Oliver North runway in front of the hotel. The hotel briefly catered to charter planeloads of Canadians from Quebec but that business was short-lived. Mostly the large hotel was devoid of guests but a full staff was always on duty and the restaurant was known for its good food, even when the dining room was empty.

The Bay Islands of Utila and Roatan

Our next destination was the Bay Islands, the end of the second longest barrier reef in the world, which runs from Belize (the old British Honduras), to Honduras. We travelled back to La Ceiba by bus then took the fifteen-minute flight to Utila, known for its diving. Utila is perhaps the cheapest place to become a certified Scuba diver, and there are numerous diving schools with well-qualified instructors from around the world. I was formerly a diver and I have dived over the Great Barrier Reef in Australia, and other major dive sites, but now I just snorkel with my wife. We snorkelled on Utila and it was quite pleasant but not brilliant compared with the Great Barrier Reef. The social life was good and there were lots of restaurants in which to hang out.

The local inhabitants of the Bay Islands are mainly descendants of Scottish and English buccaneers who once used the area plunder Spanish galleons loaded with gold. They speak English but it is hardly recognizable as such, especially when they speak amongst themselves. It is a strange, ancient sounding, sing-song dialect. The Islands used to be governed by Britain but were handed over to Honduras more than a century ago, and so the official language is now Spanish. Fortunately, for the large number of tourists the blue waters attract, English persists.

There are a few excursions you can take on Utila. One is to the only hill, which gives a great view of the island and surrounding waters, and you can imagine the pirates sailing to block unsuspecting galleons. From there you can walk to lovely sandy beaches or to mangrove swamps filled with birds and other wildlife. A short boat ride to the west took us to some tiny, uninhabited islands, which are absolutely fabulous. They were simply palm trees on golden sand surrounded by the most turquoise water imaginable. We met a couple who had camped out on one of these islands, known as Cayes, sleeping in hammocks for a week. They caught their own fish right off the beach and cooked them on an open fire. Other supplies were dropped off for them by passing fishermen from their boats. An idyllic, simple existence in paradise.

We stayed with them for a couple of hours and read our books in the shade of the palms. From the fronds above us, Pelicans were diving into the clear, blue water and coming up with an ample supply of fish. We snorkelled off the beach and it was like swimming in an aquarium. You can walk from island to island as the water is only a few feet deep, or you can snorkel between them too. One island had a house on it and it is completely self contained with its own solar cells and battery bank to run the all-electric home. In the past few years, a blight has been hitting the palm trees in the Caribbean, and Hurricane Mitch has passed through, too, so we are not sure if this paradise still exists, but it will exist in our memories forever.

We hitched a ride on a sailboat to Roatan, the largest of the islands. The wind was right behind us for the first half-hour and we made great time with jib and spinnaker full. Later there was no wind or, when there was, it was directly towards us, so we slowly motored over, enjoyed a brilliant sunset and arrived at the reef surrounding Roatan in total darkness. Our skipper knew the waters well and we glided slowly forward with flashlights shining to find a black pole indicating the narrow channel through the reef. Somehow we spotted the pole and entered the safety of the calm waters. The full moon suddenly appeared from behind a cloud and showed us the way to the dock in front of the hotel we had chosen. We were mid-way between the town of West End and the beautiful West Bay Beach, and could walk easily to these desirable destinations for food or leisure.

The snorkelling at West Bay was outstanding and we came face to face with barracuda and thousands of brilliantly coloured tropical fish as we swam through the swaying fronds of fan, brain and many other types of coral. Touring Roatan by bus, we visited Garifuna villages and passed farmland and forests. The island is well developed, yet very relaxing, as there is a holiday atmosphere everywhere. There are several up-market resorts catering to rich divers but we were most satisfied with just snorkelling.

Trujillo was still in our minds so we decided to return to see if it still had the magic that attracted us. It did, and we spent another few days looking around for property to buy. We had nearly bought some land in Costa Rica a couple of years earlier, had procrastinated, and watched the price escalate beyond our reach. This time we acted promptly and bought a small lot on the beach a few miles east of town in a new development, which we thought would be built up in just a few years. As it happens, this did not occur and the land still sits, waiting. More on the land later.

Tegucigalpa

Tegucigalpa, the capital of Honduras is a six-hour bus trip over the mountains from Trujillo through jungles and pine forests and pretty, primitive villages of mud huts. The capital is an over-populated area spread over hillsides and a valley through which runs a large, muddy sewer (actually a river). The powers that be, in their wisdom, have placed a low priority on health care in general and sewers in particular.

The state of some hospitals is deplorable and if you are not sick when you enter them, you probably will be when you leave. In one hospital (not in Tegucigalpa), I nearly stepped on a foot-high pile of used, bloody syringes and needles. They had been left alongside a septic tank waiting to be shovelled into the tank. I don't believe that stainless steel and plastic decompose very rapidly in septic tanks. The outfall of the septic field emptied onto the garbage from the prison next door and ran, in the open, down a hill to a populated area below. In the same hospital, the main electrical distribution panel was totally exposed to the elements and waiting patients--waiting to be *electrocuted*. I took photographs of the problem areas and sent them to the new Minister of Health and some action was taken, but the hospital is still a hazardous area, in my opinion.

Tegucigalpa has a huge population yet a small central area, which one can easily walk around in a few hours. There are some interesting churches and market places and the main square is always a hive of activity. Eating places abound and we found some excellent restaurants. Day trips, to the mining village of Santa Lucia and the artisans' village of Valle des Angeles, are well worth taking. The effort to find the correct bus is also worth it! The airport in Tegucigalpa (or Tegus as the locals call it) has a short runway with difficult approaches through the mountains. We flew out of Tegus to San Salvador, El Salvador, changed planes and hopped back to Guatemala City.

Guatemala

Guatemala City has little to attract, but you inevitably have to go through it when you are in Guatemala. Fortunately Antigua, our next destination, was on the same side of the city as the airport, and we were quickly out of the smog in a tourist minibus, which we shared with two American women. They had a hotel room booked, and we also stayed one night in the same hotel. It was the start of Semana Santa, or Holy Week, so towards the end of the week hotel rooms would be hard to find. We wanted to be in Antigua for the processions, which occurred each day with the climax on Good Friday. But all the hotels we checked were fully booked. We enquired of some locals in a *pulperia* (corner grocery store) and were referred to an unnamed posada near the centre. It was clean, inexpensive, had secure parking and was on the processional route--what more could we ask for?

An earthquake destroyed the old capital of Guatemala and the new capital was rebuilt on the present site of Antigua, but this was also destroyed by a major quake. Antigua had a cathedral, many churches and convents, and these were built of substantial stone. Some churches have been restored but many buildings remain as ruins and a reminder of the powerful quake. Buildings that survived the earthquake are arranged in a regular grid pattern on cobbled streets, and the architecture is colonial Spanish. When walking around you can get frequent glimpses of courtyards filled with colourful Bougainvillaea and fountains in the old haciendas and posadas.

The city is dominated to the south by the perfect cone of a volcano, another constant reminder of the fragility of life in the city. On the side of the volcano are small villages whose inhabitants harvest their crops from the fertile volcanic soil, seemingly oblivious to possible danger. The Indian inhabitants of the villages produce beautiful, brightly coloured weavings, which are sold in their local markets. They also bring their handiwork to the market and streets of Antigua. The Catholic Church in the centre of each village dominates the village and there they mix their animism with Catholicism. The craft market in Antigua is a blaze of bright reds, blues, oranges and yellows made into shawls, wall hangings and clothes.

It is hard to resist buying one of each. The same colours are used in the carpets for the processions.

During Easter Week, Antigua fills with people and anticipation. Floats depicting the procession prior to Christ's crucifixion are prepared in the churches. Nearly every day is a procession day for one church or another. On the particular processional route for the day, a carpet of coloured sawdust and flowers and pine needles is laid in intricate designs on the cobbled stones.

Each house or business fronting the route is responsible for a section of carpet and many hours are spent on laying the complicated carpets. The carpets will be destroyed by the hundreds of men and women carrying the floats in the procession. Accompanying the floats are people burning incense, while a band of drums, trumpets and tubas play mournful dirges. The route is lined with thousands of tourists and visitors, mainly from Latin American countries.

On Good Friday, several processions take place simultaneously from different churches on different routes, which occasionally cross each other. They are proceeded by an early morning gallop of Roman soldiers on horseback through the streets. The whole spectacle is a bizarre symbolism gone crazy. We would not have missed it for anything, but by the end of the week we were processioned out. On Easter Sunday we went to the Indian mountain town of Chichicastenango where a huge market for woven goods and food is held weekly. Easter Day has a special market, and a parade of people and religious artefacts passes around the main square where the goods are sold, causing canopies to be removed and replaced as the procession passes through. At the same time, pipe bombs are set off with enormous bangs, frightening all within a mile. It's yet another bizarre event and a great photo opportunity.

Lake Atitlan is a huge crater lake on the shores of which are situated charming Indian villages. We drove from Chichicastenango to Panajachel, otherwise known as Gringotenango, at the north end of the lake. From there, we took one of the frequent ferries that ply around Lake Atitlan to Santa Cruz. We stayed several nights in a comfortable small lakeside hotel run by one of the many gringos. Some people swam in the lake but the waters were a bit chilly for me. I have to be able to enter water without flinching before I consider it swimmable.

The setting is dramatic with an enormous, perfectly shaped volcano on the opposite side of the lake. The altitude is quite high, even on the lakeside, so the nights are cool and the days a very pleasant, warm temperature. Travellers often pass through the villages in the area, as they are on a well-travelled and popular route in Guatemala. As a result, there is ample opportunity for the exchange of information on where to stay and places to go. We ran into the same travellers several times in different villages on the lake.

At the south end of the lake is Santiago Atitlan, which boasts a large market and church. People from many outlying villages come to Santiago for commerce and worship. Both the men and women still wear their traditional costumes; the men wearing what look like baseball uniforms with striped trousers. Many carried the tool of the peasants' trade, a large hoe. Men and women would both balance enormous loads of produce or firewood on their heads, or they would wear traditional hats whose shapes and colours identified their home villages. Again it was cold at night, but our hotel bedroom had a fireplace that kept us cosy.

One day we went for a long walk, which took us past a memorial to a large number of villagers who had been slaughtered by the army a year or two earlier. It was a grim reminder to us of the recent violent past when civil war tore apart the country. We did not feel in any danger ourselves and were greeted by friendly waves and smiles wherever we went. There were no other travellers on the beautiful trail through forests and jungles to a mountain ridge, which gave us panoramic views over the lake.

After three days in Santiago Atitlan, we took the ferry directly back to Panajachel where we stopped to check out the many market stalls on the roads in the town. It is a great place to shop for Indian weavings and crafts and we wished we had more room in our packs for the tempting bargains available. Sadly, we had to leave the beautiful weavings behind us, but we resolved to come that way again on our future travels.

With some trepidation, we took a bus to Guatemala City. Having heard several travellers' reports of robberies from tourists, we found a secure hotel not far from the bus station. We safely walked around the central areas in daylight but were not particularly impressed by the city. It was busy, grubby and polluted with gas and diesel fumes generated by the frantic traffic. Back near our hotel, we ran into a Canadian man whom we had met in Trujillo three weeks earlier; he was returning from the bus station where he had been relieved of his back pack while he waited for his bus to leave. He stood at the front door at the same time as his pack exited by the back door. The pack contained his passport and money and he was not happy. We always keep our valuables in a concealed money belt around our waists in case of such an eventuality.

The following day, we were especially careful when we walked the short distance to the same bus station. A group of youths offered to carry our packs, which of course we were quite capable of carrying, but they helpfully escorted us to the bus. Our destination was Chiquimula, on the way to the Honduran border. Our large packs were safely stowed on the racks overhead and Noreen carried her small daypack containing a guidebook, some pills and a snack.

A man, who looked like the driver or his assistant, was helping people aboard while standing near the driver's seat at the front of the bus. He indicated to Noreen that she should place her pack on the rack above her with our large packs. When she resisted, he insisted that it would be perfectly safe and in fact, was a police requirement. We didn't quite buy that, but to keep the peace, she placed the pack directly overhead and kept her eye on it. While a food vendor distracted me outside my window, there was a loud argument at the front of the bus, which caught Noreen's attention for a second. In that second, the daypack disappeared. Noreen, who is normally a quiet and calm person, jumped up yelling that her pack was gone. A group of youths hurriedly left the front door of the bus but did not have her pack with them, as far as we could tell. Meanwhile, I was still looking around on the overhead rack, when two ladies behind us pointed to a seat several rows behind us on the bus. There lay Noreen's pack, waiting to be passed out of the window. We were very fortunate, but it did give us a

We had to change to a minibus in Chiquimula. The driver asked us to place our bags on the outside rack but we were determined to keep our large packs with us on the bus. In fact I became quite rude and obnoxious to the driver and swore at him, which is not my normal nature. We won the battle and the passengers had to squeeze a little tighter around our bulky packs. They were very good-natured about it, and I felt sorry for reacting the way I did. People in the countryside are very different from the city folk.

Our destination that night was Esquipulas near the border, and we would get an early bus the following morning. Esquipulas is a pretty little town, known by Catholics for artefacts in the main church in the square. It was quiet the day we were there but we could see the elaborate queuing arrangements they would put in place for the important festivals to which thousands of people would flock to see the artefacts.

Return to Honduras

The border crossing at Agua Calientes into Honduras is not a pleasant place, but we were not held up unduly on that occasion and made the transfer to a Honduran bus with ease. It is at times like this that we found our *Lonely Planet* book invaluable, as it tells you all the tricks to make the bus connections easily. That day, we were able to take five buses (without speaking Spanish), cross the border into Honduras, and make our way to the tiny town of Gracias.

Gracias is in the hills near Santa Rosa de Copan and is near to the Celaque National Park to which we hiked the next day. It was a long, hot hike but took us through interesting farmland and forest and ended in the park. Celaque was very lush and supposed to contain many wild animals and birds. Unfortunately, the wildlife decided to hide from us and we were disappointed; the hike however was invigorating and scenic. It was only a few short bus rides to the Mayan ruins at Copan Ruinas, and we spent several days exploring the town, the ruins and the surrounding countryside.

The town of Copan itself is small and compact with the usual central square. A number of hotels and restaurants cater to tourists visiting the ruins or taking one of the many Spanish courses offered in the town. The ruins themselves are magnificent, and we caught them on a day when there were only a few visitors. We were able to clamber over the sixteen hundred-year-old rocks so carefully carved and placed by the old civilization of the Mayas. There are still archaeologists exploring and excavating the tunnels in the tombs, and a museum has been built to house artefacts and to explain the meaning of the ancient scripts on the monuments.

A good way to get the feel of the Mayan environment is to trek through the countryside on horseback. You can mount your horse in the main square or outside your hotel and quickly ride into the quiet country. You might come across several carved rock outcrops in unexpected places as you traverse the fields, rivers and hills of the area and imagine the Mayan Indians working their fields. No one seems to be sure what happened to the Mayans in 800 A.D. It is possible that the valley became overpopulated and could not produce the food required or perhaps some disease swept the area.

Visiting Copan was a sweet way to finish our tour of Guatemala and Honduras, and the good memories took us back many times in the following years. A happy couple, we flew back to Vancouver by way of San Pedro Sula, El Salvador and Los Angeles.

Chapter 7

Honduras, Our Second Home

A Dream Home

The town of Trujillo on the Caribbean, north coast, of Honduras has become our second home. We had bought a small piece of land on the beach on our first visit to the area and later went about the task of designing a house. This would fulfil our desire for a winter home for two or three months a year. The rest of the time we hoped to rent it out so that the economics would make sense.

With the help of John Eaves, an architect friend in Vancouver, we designed our two-bedroom house with a large living area giving a wonderful view of the ocean. A balcony off the master bedroom offered a magnificent view of the mountains and National Park to the south. The working drawings were prepared for us by an architect in Trujillo who made use of locally available building materials and specified construction methods known to local contractors. Designing for the tropical climate is quite different from designing for temperate zones. You have to consider huge amounts of rain, the odd hurricane, heat and sun, as well as the corrosive salty environment. We thought we had done a pretty good job and started to get prices for construction. This was easier said than done, and the contractors' prices covered quite a range. It was obvious that they could not do a proper estimate of materials or labour so we gave them a list of materials. Even then, there was a wide variation in prices. We tried to qualify potential builders based on their previous work in the area, but we found that none of them came without complaints from their clients.

The one piece of advice, given by all the previous people who had houses built for them, was to be sure that we were on site for the whole of the construction period. We had spent several months on the bidding and selection process and, at the same time, were trying to get the American developer to provide water to the site, as he had promised. The developer, a lawyer, was more interested in building his own house in a different part of town and socializing with his young friends. He failed to get the promised wells drilled, holding tank built and distribution system installed. We decided to abandon the idea of starting construction that year.

We geared ourselves up to come the following year and stay for six months to complete the house.

In Vancouver we selected the vehicle we wanted to take to Honduras. It was to be a totally rebuilt 1985 Toyota 4 Runner to give us the leaf spring suspension and lift recommended for Central American roads. We had a heavy-duty roof rack installed to carry building supplies for the house, as we had found out that most contractors in Trujillo don't even have a truck.

We attended garage sales frequently and assembled all the appliances, pots, pans, crockery and cutlery we would need, and which could not be bought locally in Honduras. We consulted guidebooks for the trip down and found that there was a ferry direct to Honduras from Brownsville, Texas.

We tried to book our passage with the truck, but this was not easy. The ferry had broken down and was in dry dock for repairs. We had a back-up plan to drive through Mexico and Guatemala if the ferry was not repaired in time. As we were driving to Honduras through the U.S.A., we heard that the ferry was running again, and we headed for Brownsville at the southernmost tip of Texas. The ferry was quite acceptable with pleasant cabins and cafeteria, but the weather was most unpleasant. The ship rolled its way across the Gulf of Mexico causing many a green face among the passengers. The weather worsened and the captain sought the shelter of the island of Cozumel off Cancun on the Yucatan Peninsula of Mexico.

We arrived in Puerto Cortez, Honduras, a day late on our four day cruise and, of course, there was just time to unload the cars before the customs office closed for the day. We found the least grotty hotel and holed-up for the night, arriving early the next morning to start the paper work to clear the car and goods through customs. This required the help of an agent. The agent kept disappearing on us throughout the day, coming back briefly every few hours to ask for more money for each document that was processed. At the end of the day, we were not too much further ahead than we had been the day before, but we were a lot poorer.

We had to spend another night in that miserable hotel and turn up at customs again in the morning. The paper work seemed to be complete by lunchtime, and at that time, a friend we had run into introduced us to the head of customs. I took the opportunity of telling her what I thought of their system and received sympathetic noises. But by then we were on our way, we thought.

There remained one more hurdle to cross--the final inspection. Our truck was jammed full of stuff for our house, and we were well over our limit for the importation of duty-free goods. Fortunately the chief of customs, whom we had met earlier, saw our load of stuff and realized we would be stuck even longer, so she took us into an office and stamped our passport with a special exemption. It pays to complain sometimes. After a further delay at the gate, because the guard had gone to lunch, we started our drive along the north coast towards Trujillo.

The roads were not bad, mostly paved, but with some truck-eating potholes that occurred when you least expected them. There were numerous bridges with bumps at both ends of them, but no rivers to ford. We stopped in the town of La Ceiba, which is the third largest city in the country, checked into a hotel, and went out for pizza at Pizza Hut. It was to be our last chance to eat North American food for a few months. The final leg of our journey to Trujillo the next morning took us over decidedly worse roads. The province of Colon seems to be ignored by the central government, or maybe the funds are misappropriated, but it feels as if one is entering a depressed area at the end of the road from civilization. In spite of this, we like Trujillo and were excited to be returning to build our house.

It was still the rainy season but we wanted to be early to ensure the building would go well once we started. The wretched developer still hadn't got the water tank finished, so we hassled him and were promised it was just weeks away. We decided to unload our effects from the truck and drive on down to Costa Rica for Christmas and the New Year, returning in January to start building. That journey is part of another chapter in our travels.

In January, the water tank was filled but the bottom fell out. We couldn't start to build without water and it would be weeks before there would be any. We would have to abandon thoughts of building for another year. I was determined to do something though so I started to take cuttings from Bougainvillaea plants for a fence. People gave me mango and ginger plants, which I started to nurse along at our rental apartment property. I bought thirty palm trees and planted them around our land. The living fence, I had erected when we first arrived, had started to grow and the landscaping was progressing even if the house was not.

By the end of April, the developer had repaired the tank but the underground piping had leaked badly and the main valve had broken. There was still no water and my plants would die if I planted them without watering them. I arranged for someone to take care of them at another location until we returned the following year to try again to build.

Medical Missions

In the meantime, we learned that two medical missions were coming to work in Trujillo and in surrounding villages, so we volunteered to work with them. I could drive our truck and Noreen could use her nursing skills. The first group operated at a clinic they had built in Chapagua, a village in the Aguan Valley, some distance out of town, Noreen worked there as a nurse in triage. I drove the truck and delivered people and supplies as required. We enjoyed our work and our association with the group, who came from all parts of the U.S.A. and Canada. I made a video of their activities and was asked to produce many copies for the volunteers to take home. I hope the video helped them to gain support for future missions. We have now worked with this group on three of their missions and have come to know and like them very much.

We all get emotionally involved in some of the more serious cases. One such case was a thirteen-year-old girl called Sonja, who had given birth to a baby boy a month earlier. She had brought the baby to see a doctor, as the baby was not getting the nourishment it required. The baby was almost lifeless and very anaemic, as was her mother. Both mother and baby were treated in the clinic. Sonja refused hospitalization, which was recommended by the doctors, as she had no money for transportation or treatment.

The following day, we decided to try once again to persuade the girl to take the baby for hospital treatment. I set off with an interpreter to find Sonja in the village she had named when she checked in at the clinic. But after a search we realized that she must have come from another village. We drove around four other villages asking for someone who knew the girl, and finally, after much detective work, we tracked her down to a simple, bare concrete-block house where she was sitting on the floor, feeding her baby. The baby's bed was a plastic potato sack hung from the roof with string. Clothes were in cardboard boxes and there was little or no food in the kitchen. The baby was still a very bad colour and was limp. When my interpreter held the tiny baby in her arms, she felt that there was only a little life left in the child. I told Sonja that we were taking her and the child to hospital immediately, and she meekly agreed.

We drove very quickly over awful roads for nearly an hour, and they were admitted at once to the emergency paediatric ward where a team of nurses and a doctor evaluated and treated them both. The baby received a blood transfusion, as it appeared he had contracted malaria from his mother just prior to his birth. We gave Sonja money for all her immediate needs and she stayed in hospital for several days. The young mother was a child herself and had little clue how to care for her own child. We had learned on our speedy trip to the hospital that Sonja's mother had died a week earlier, and that her father was living in a town faraway. There was no one at home to teach or help her. We arranged for help in the form of food, clothes and emotional support from a missionary group and pray that mother Sonja and baby Saul will pull through.

The Chapagua Clinic Group also identified several children with major deformities who might be able to benefit from medical help in the United States. I took two of these children to a clinic in the town of Tocoa for X-rays. I sadly watched a small boy, Jairo, with only two fingers and a thumb on each hand as he patiently laid his poor hands in different positions for the exposures. One of Jairo's feet was rotated a hundred and eighty degrees from the other. The other child, Iris, was a lovely looking ten-year-old with badly bowed legs. Her infirmity was tragic but her smile was devastating. We hope that sponsors are found to fly the patients to the U.S.A. and that doctors will offer to perform the operations free of charge. Foster parents will have to be found to house and care for Jairo and Iris during the long, stressful recovery process.

The second medical group came from Arkansas and numbered over ninety members of the congregation of a church. They consisted of doctors, nurses, engineers, contractors and a dozen other professionals. They brought equipment and medicines by the container-load and were well organized. There is always room for extra help, and Noreen and I spent an arduous week working in several outlying clinics and in the main hospital in Trujillo. Again we thoroughly enjoyed ourselves and met some very interesting and dedicated people with whom we are still in touch. The group is from a Roman Catholic Church and is quite religious. They like to evangelize and we have a hard time with this, as we are not at all religious. Our assistance to the group is purely humanitarian.

We met hundreds of Hondurans from extremely poor villages and who were suffering all kinds of ailments; many were under nourished. Medicine was dispensed by the truckload--and vitamins too. They were appreciative of the aid being given and we received lots of smiles. Operations were performed on cleft palates and deformed limbs. One child had six digits on each hand

and foot and had the extras removed. Another man arrived at the hospital with a bandaged wrist; when a nurse undid the bandage, the hand fell off. Doctors could not reattach the hand but the patient was cleaned up and sent home.

Many wounds were from machetes, some by accidents and some the result of acts of violence. A man lost both his hands to a machete blow when he made a pass at another man's wife; the wife only lost one hand. A boy cut his foot with a machete while working in the fields and had to walk five miles to the clinic where he required twenty stitches. He was ready to walk home but the doctor knew the stitches would all be pulled if he did so. I was called upon to drive him home in the truck, and we crossed rivers and travelled along cart tracks until we reached a small mud hut where he lived with his parents and ten siblings in one room without water or power.

Lots of patients were coughing, some had tuberculosis, some had malaria or dengue fever. Noreen and I had vaccinations for everything and were taking malaria prophylactics, but we both came down with flu symptoms later. Fortunately, for us, they were innocuous, and we recovered quickly.

The rest of our time in Trujillo was taken up with relaxing on the beach and by my daily English class for six of the poor children in the area. I figured it would be much easier for these four children to learn English than for an old man like me to learn Spanish. In any case, it would be a good idea to give these underprivileged children a little advantage over the more wealthy ones.

We returned to Vancouver in our truck, disappointed that our building project was stalled again

but satisfied that we had done a little to help many less
fortunate than ourselves.

Hurricane Mitch

In November 1998, Hurricane Mitch struck Honduras.
The eye of the storm hovered over one of the Bay islands
just offshore from Trujillo and spilled rain over the area
for days. Hurricane-force winds blew off roofs, rain
dissolved the mud walls, and many houses were lost. No
lives were lost in Trujillo but in remote areas many lost
their lives or homes. The banana and pineapple crops
were devastated, as were almost all other plantations.
Bridges and roads washed out; power and telephone lines
went down. Some eight thousand people died and over a
million were homeless in Honduras. We heard it all on
CNN and by e-mail from friends while we were leading a
group to Bali. Fortunately, all our friends in Trujillo were
alive.

When we returned to Vancouver from Indonesia in
December 1998, we immediately collected money and
assembled as many relief supplies as we could muster
from friends. We attended garage sales and bought and
solicited goods too. Our truck was prepared for the long
trip back to Honduras as, by this time, the ferry was
cancelled permanently and we had to drive all the way.

In mid January 1999, we set off through the United
States, visiting friends and collecting more money on the
way. We were a little upset by Honduran customs at the
border in Aqua Calientes, who charged us duty on the
relief supplies we had brought down, but this was Central
America, after all. We placed bundles of clothes in sacks

and arranged for them to be sent into remote mountain villages on horseback and distributed by missionaries to the needy.

Other clothes, goods and food we handed out ourselves directly to people who had been the hardest hit. Among these, were people in the village of Santa Rosa de Aguan on the edge of the Mosquito Coast. They were not directly in Mitch's path but were hit by major floods from water dumped in the centre of the country over several days. The water destroyed homes, a school and roads, making the town unrecognizable to us, even though we had been there only nine months previously. We saw two school buses buried in the river mud and sand.

With the money we had collected, four frames for homes were built for families, who had lost theirs in the hurricane. Each frame consisted of four posts, a corrugated metal roof, two windows and a door. The family had to erect the walls using sticks and mud in the traditional manner or built the walls using wood, concrete-blocks or metal. We had selected the families ourselves with the help of Carlos Hernandez, the administrator of the poor children's school, and he had arranged for the purchase of materials and the labour for construction. We used our truck to carry the construction materials to the different home sites. In all, we provided homes for thirty persons in these primitive circumstances.

When our projects were complete, I continued my new career as a teacher, this time teaching a class of forty-four children and several teachers and parents. It was a lot of fun, the students learned some English, and I learned some Spanish, too. I still find Spanish difficult but I do understand enough to get by on a day to day basis for the ordering of food and beer.

Hurricane Mitch changed Trujillo in several ways, not least of which was the overall economy in the town. Suddenly there was no income for those who relied on farm crops or who worked for the port. There were no tourists in town and the locals had no money to spend with merchants; cash flow slowed to a trickle. The only saving grace was the influx of medical, clothes and food aid from other countries. The economy also received a boost from providing the accommodation required for the soldiers and volunteers from Canada, U.S.A., Britain, Ireland and Sweden. Unfortunately, some of the donated goods wound up in a local supermarket and restaurant and were being sold for the profit of a leading local politician. Clothes were also pilfered from containers by government officials and sent out to their wealthy friends who had no need for relief.

Foreign soldiers were much in evidence on the roads in their "Hummers" and they organized the replacement of roads, culverts and bridges. It was evident that some of the roads were very poorly built in the first place. We saw areas where the road base had been washed away, revealing an asphalt layer no more than two inches thick, and this was for roads with continuous container truck traffic. Soon all areas were accessible and the infrastructure of the country was back to the way it was before the hurricane. No tourists appeared, however, as the stories of devastation have kept them away even three years later.

Other changes were evident after Mitch. Relationships between people in the town changed and those who were friends before the hurricane no longer spoke to one another. We were not there ourselves during those difficult times and can only guess at the stress that everybody was under and the way people reacted. Some of the damage was permanent but other relationships have developed as the ex-patriot community is small and they have to get on reasonably well to survive.

It is said that in Central America, many of the ex-pats are either wanted by the law or not wanted by society. We know of one man who used to have a large marijuana grow operation in California. Others simply do not like paying taxes in their home country. The characters in town are diverse, and you can be whomever you wish and make up your own background. This is evident when one hears the claims of some, who purport to be professional people, when it is obvious that they are not. I was guilty of that myself on one occasion.

I was stopped at a major roadblock during an illegal land claim by displaced villagers one day and our car papers and my passport had been left in our house by mistake. I had been to a remote community delivering doctors and nurses to a clinic, and I was alone in the vehicle. In my terrible Spanish, I told the police that I was working with a medical group from Canada. In retrospect, I suspect that I actually told them I was a doctor myself. Anyway, the explanation worked and I was allowed through the roadblock.

Land occupations were not uncommon after Mitch. Squatters appeared in all kinds of places, such as road medians outside San Pedro Sula, an abandoned army base near Trujillo, and private land everywhere. Those who had lost their homes, or whose villages were still under water, would erect shanties and the Honduran flag, and try to claim the land as their own. Usually the police and army would move them on after a few days, or the local authority would find them an alternative site and the claimants would go peacefully. It was quite intimidating to see so many guns in the hands of such young policemen and soldiers as they faced a dishevelled group of campesinos whose only weapons were sticks and machetes.

The prevalence of firearms in Honduras is so alien to my background from England and Canada. There are millions of guns in Honduras, and they are used frequently. We have been offered them on several occasions but we always answer that we do not "do" guns. Some Americans and other foreigners bring them into the country, smuggling them inside kitchen appliances and washing machines. Sometimes they bribe a customs agent not to inspect their effects when they enter the country. We saw someone sawing off the barrel of a shotgun right in the bar of a local restaurant. One gringo in town, a retired prison guard, has offered to give the women lessons in the use of their 45's--its as if when you have a gun you must be prepared to use it as a deadly weapon.

One night, we were awakened by nine loud reports near our house. Noreen thought they were firecrackers but I assured her they were not. It turned out that two guards were exchanging fire, apparently in an ongoing personal dispute. One of the guards had previously been imprisoned for killing a man and was now the security guard for an orphanage. The logic of the orphanage was that it was good to have a bad man on your side. Most of the Americans, including women, carry guns with them, and some routinely discharge their weapons before they go to bed; just to let their neighbours and others know they are armed and prepared. One woman never moves without her gun, even when she drives the two hundred yards from her house to a tennis court. Many of them live in large houses with bars on their windows, an armed guard and a roaming guard dog patrolling the gated grounds and barbed wire fences.

All this may seem normal to my American friends and readers but to me, that is no way to live--in constant fear that you will be robbed or attacked. We may be naive, but we do not have that fear. We are sensible about what we wear--that is, no jewellery, expensive watches, visible wallets or purses, and we stick to well-lighted streets at night. We greet the locals with a smile and an "Adios," "Hola," or "Buenos Dias," and are always greeted in return. Noreen would run alone through all areas of town on every street during her early morning exercise with no fear or apprehension. We feel safer in Trujillo than we would in any city in the U.S.A. It is a small town of mixed races: Hispanic, Garifuna, Indian, European and North American and they all live in harmony and with tolerance. There are robberies and occasional acts of violence but there are more muggings every night in big cities all over the world than in Trujillo in a year.

The justice system in Honduras is based on the Napoleonic system, which differs greatly from the British and American systems. For example, after an accident, everyone involved is liable to be thrown into jail until his innocence is proved. Several gringos have found themselves in jail and have been bailed out by rich friends--it does pay to have money. The legal process can be very slow but sometimes it is accelerated by people who take the law into their own hands.

On one occasion, a Honduran woman, who had been assaulted many times by her husband, was nearly killed by him. A friend of hers took it upon himself to beat the husband until he was dead and to throw his body into a river. No-one bothered to follow up on the case as the consensus was that justice had been done. When an American serviceman was killed for his money, many people knew the perpetrator but were afraid to testify against him. The police, allegedly, sought out the man and killed him in the jungle.

Another mystery surrounds the death of a European woman who was buried by her husband within twenty-four hours of her death. He himself died mysteriously a year later, leaving his house, not to his family, but to people whom he hardly knew. They are prominent and wealthy Hondurans. His house was found to contain precious artefacts that were stolen from a Peruvian museum and worth a fortune.

Legendary "Bill"

We have a good friend in Trujillo whom we have known since our very first trip to the country. I shall call him Bill. Bill used to run a very successful bar that was "The" place to go for conversation with other travellers, and he was the source of a wealth of information on the area. He took us on a trip to Santa Rosa de Aguan on the edge of the Mosquitia region on the eastern north coast. We rode in the back of his pick-up truck through rivers and along terrible unpaved roads to the little town at the mouth of the Rio Aguan.

The town is split in two by the river, and you cross by dugout canoe. Before we crossed over, Bill ordered a meal from a home and asked that it be ready for us on our return in about an hour. On the other side, we wandered through delightful dusty streets with especially friendly people; some were Garifuna, some Indian and some Hispanic. They all seemed to speak several languages including a little English. The beach was over a sand-dune from the houses and was a long, beautiful, empty stretch of sand with waves crashing on the shore. Four curious children accompanied us on our walk along the otherwise deserted sands, and the whole scene was idyllic.

Back on the other side of the river, lunch was being prepared, and when we got back to the house, wonderful smells were emanating from the little kitchen. Not fish smells but wood smoke and coconut. We were invited into the living room and sat at a table laid for six. Our group included Bill, his wife, her sister and a guide we had picked up in the town. We were served beer and then a magnificent pot of langostinas cooked in coconut milk. We have never tasted anything quite as good either before or since. Langostinas are a freshwater crustacean, better than lobster. We all tucked in to the pot and more langostinas were brought until we could eat no more. I was feeling pretty well after the beautiful broth, succulent meat and beer and I offered to pay the whole bill. I need not have been concerned by my apparent generosity, for the total was only eighteen dollars U.S.

I started with a good story about Bill, but all the others surrounding him are legendary for their disastrous features. One night he was driving home from the bar and noticed a prowler in his garage. He felt for his gun and took quick aim to fire a warning shot at the man. Now most people fire warning shots into the air--but not Bill, who managed to shoot a hole in the windshield of his truck!

On a several day trip into the Mosquitia region, Bill was on a boat in the ocean off Patuca Point with the captain, six crewmen and a man from Guanaja. This man claimed he knew the location of a sunken Spanish galleon, which allegedly had a fortune of gold on board. It became obvious that they had been led on a wild goose chase, and the man and Bill got into an argument that ended in blows. The blows developed into a machete attack on Bill, which sent him overboard with the man in pursuit.

The captain circled the boat around the feuding pair and plucked them out of the water, sending each of them to opposite ends of the boat to cool off. After a tense dinner, the man took his turn at the helm. At eight o'clock in the evening, Bill went to the stern to relieve himself but was seen by the helmsman who apparently swung the wheel sharply, causing Bill to fall overboard. The boat carried on, leaving Bill in the water dressed only in his Guatemalan shorts, while the helmsman did not trouble to raise the alarm.

When the others finally noticed Bill's absence, Bill was far behind and a search for him was fruitless. Meanwhile, Bill used his shorts as an airbag flotation device and treaded water, as he had no idea of the direction of land. From 8:00 P.M. until 4:30 A.M. he was stationary in the water. At first light, he could make out the shoreline some eight miles away. It was an all-day swim, but Bill finally made it to the beach, totally exhausted. He thought his time was up when night fell.

Somehow he hung on and some Mosquitia Indians spotted him the following morning and took him back to their village. Bill was in pretty bad shape, mainly from dehydration and sunburn. The Indians looked after him very well. His friends from the boat decided to search the shore for Bill's body but instead found him alive and well, sleeping in a hammock attended by his caregivers.

Another story is told of how Bill took a group of tourists fishing in the bay. The boat sank, leaving the tourists to swim for shore. The boat and a brand new motor wound up at the bottom of the sea.

On one of our first trips to Trujillo, we had been sitting at the Bahia Bar and were starting to walk back to our hotel when two men in a pick-up truck gave us a lift. We passed the local gas station and noticed a crowd hanging around but did not stop. It turned out that there had just been a hold-up and an armed gunman had stolen the day's takings. The hold-up had been witnessed by our friend, Bill, who had driven on into town to pick up the police who, at that time, had no transportation of their own. They drove back to the gas station to find that the gunman had taken a hostage and was running across a field nearby. The gunman opened fire on Bill and the police in the back of his truck but fortunately he had a very bad aim and he failed to hit even the truck. The police also opened fire but missed their mark and then ran out of bullets. The gunman escaped into the jungle leaving the hostage shaken but unharmed.

Bill's bar, the *Rincon de Los Amigos*, used to be a going concern, often filled with locals and visitors during the day and really buzzing at night, especially at weekends when he would bring in live bands for rock and *punta* dancing. *Punta* is the traditional Garifuna dance with an African beat from drums and turtle shells, with the sound from a conch shell heard over the beat. Bill had a great collection of posters and flags from many nations in the bar, and there were seats and tables both inside and on the beach in front. One of the drinks for which the bar was famous was a pina colada, served in a whole pineapple and delivered to your table with a burning sparkler.

Bill's partner was a trifle merry one night and was dancing on the tables with a burning sparkler when he accidentally set fire to the thatched roof of the bar. The ensuing blaze engulfed the bar in flames and destroyed the valuable collection of posters and flags. The partner sold his share in the bar to an Irishman from New York and the bar was rebuilt and continued to thrive.

When Mitch hit, the bar's roof was damaged, its furniture destroyed and the whole place filled with many tons of sand. What little remained was stolen. There was no money for rebuilding and the bar was abandoned until the police chief decided to claim it and have the sand removed by some of the prisoners from the jail. After a short court battle, Bill regained control and now the bar is being leased to a family who is starting to get it going again.

Unfortunately, few visitors come to town as a result of the publicity about Mitch, and all businesses are struggling just to stay alive. Bill has another job out of town and is saving to finish building his house. His house was a victim of an attack when a group of youths entered, firing their guns. Bill found twenty-two bullet holes in the kitchen. The house was empty except for a young boy who was hit in the chest; by a miracle, the bullet passed straight through without causing significant damage. The house was cleaned of valuables. On a neighbour's property the following morning, the police found all the stolen goods, covered in human excrement. In spite of all these disasters, and a few untold ones, Bill continues to live and read voraciously in his home in this special Caribbean beach town.

Tales of Trujillo

Trujillo has a fine airstrip, courtesy of Ollie North, although it is unfenced and beginning to deteriorate as nobody has maintained it since Ollie left. Locals use it as a roadway to the beach bars and houses along the beach. It is also used by grazing cattle, loose horses, donkeys, dogs and people. It is a great place to have driving lessons, too. The American and Honduran warplanes don't use the strip very often, and generally only American helicopters drop in once a month on training exercises. The thing that worries us is the hazards posed to the regularly scheduled commercial flights, which arrive several times a day.

We frequently hear the roar of engines as planes abort their landings when a cow or vehicle strays into their path just before the landing. There is no warning of an imminent landing, and once I glanced in my rear view mirror to see a plane landing, and I had to pull off to the side rather sharply. Noreen was about to charge into a plane taking off until a taxi, also coming towards her, flashed his lights in warning, yelling "Avion, Avion!" That plane happened to be carrying someone important, and there were soldiers at the other end of the runway with machine guns. None of them considered the possibility of cars driving into the path of the plane from the road at the opposite end. One of these days there will be a crash and then the powers that be will think about erecting a fence around the runway and making it into an airport rather than a joint use facility.

We have been to four weddings in our few times in Trujillo, and I have taken the photos and videos for all of them. That was the reason we were invited, I suppose. We found them all enjoyable in different ways, but the most interesting one was held in a tiny collection of mud huts in the mountains near the town.

There was no electricity in the hamlet, but a generator was brought in for the occasion and provided power for lights and music and a public address system for the church itself, which was also a mud hut. The service started at seven in the evening and consisted of dozens of people getting up to say a few words, reading from the Bible or leading a hymn or song. The people of the hamlet, numbering about a hundred, were all in attendance and all related to one another and to the bride. The groom was an ex-patriot Englishman, and his best "man" was an American woman. We did not find out which speaker was the minister until hours later--they were all so enthusiastic as they loudly sang their hallelujahs.

Finally, after two and a half hours, the real minister, a Mennonite from a neighbouring Garifuna village, started to read the actual wedding ceremony and vows were given and rings exchanged. The combination of Evangelical and Mennonite rites made for quite a bizarre event that lasted for longer than I care to remember.

Most of the gringos in town stick to themselves and do not mix much with the locals. The exception would be at a Chamber of Commerce function when everyone important attends. One gringo has made a project of installing lighting in schools and we have helped him on a couple of schools. Others turn out when missionary groups come to town to conduct medical clinics, and they act as interpreters. Apart from these contacts, most of the gringos live in their fancy homes attended by local maids, gardeners and security guards who open and close gates for them. There are some gringo men who have taken young Honduran girls as wives or girlfriends. When I say young, I mean really young--sometimes they are only teenagers taken by fifty-plus year-olds.

There is a story of a gringo who bought a cigarette boat in the Florida Keyes, filled it with spare parts for cars and other effects, with the idea of bringing the boat and goods into Honduras. I wondered if he intended to pay the duty. The first time he left with a friend from Key West, the boat broke down and they had to return to the dock. The second attempt took them to Cuba, but they were immediately arrested and the boat searched. The gringo was reprimanded for not flying the Cuban, U.S. or quarantine flags, but when he tried to buy an American flag, there were none available--surprise! He seemed to forget that there has been a cold war going on for years and his anger with the officials and threats to call his embassy had little effect. He also thought that a credit card would buy him gas at the marina, and he had to pay with his limited cash, which only bought enough gas for the boat to return to Key West.

The boat left Key West several more times, returning because of engine trouble, and finally reached a point 120 miles north of Roatan, Honduras, where both engines completely stopped. The boat drifted for a couple of days, although the gringo claims he was in total control the whole time. "I was doing my captain thing!" he later told me. A passing banana boat stopped and then radioed for help as the small boat's radio was not working properly, and finally a Mexican Navy ship took the powerless craft under tow to the island of Cozumel on the Yucatan Peninsula. The gringo and his friend left the boat to be repaired and returned to Trujillo.

After several weeks and two trips back to Cozumel, they left again for Honduras and this time broke down off Belize. Again they drifted for days before being rescued and towed into Belize. When we last heard, the boat engines were still under repair and the contraband still on board.

We have made two return trips from Trujillo to Tegucigalpa, the capital of Honduras, and taken various routes through the mountains. This has been contrary the advice of some, including our Honduran lawyers, who feel that these are dangerous roads to travel. True, there have been a few incidences of hold-ups, one of a busload of locals, who were told to strip to their underwear by a gang of thugs, who made off with their clothes. Another time, a missionary escaped with his life and that of his family, after he had stopped to help a fellow motorist. The motorist was apparently in distress but instead demanded that the missionary hand over his gun. The missionary refused--even though he had no gun--and the motorist shot him in the leg.

We decided we would not stop for anyone and would count on our sturdy truck to get us through, which it did. The roads were mostly in good shape, although none were paved, and they carried us through most spectacular scenery. We tried to traverse one mountain range on a road shown dotted on the map but failed when it deteriorated into a narrow trail along a cliff. We had to retrace our path and this caused us to be delayed significantly, forcing us to stay overnight in a village high in the mountains.

The hotels were all much the same, somewhat grotty and with paper-thin walls and an abundance of spiders and cockroaches. We were pleased to leave at first light and head for home. Later, we heard that the village had been a feuding ground for two families who would regularly dispense with their opposite numbers. They had recently made a pact and had ceremoniously buried all their weapons --well at least the rusty ones.

I hope all this talk of poverty and violence will not put people off going to Honduras. With common sense, one can safely live in this beautiful country where the tropical climate is most conducive to an easy lifestyle. One should stay in Honduras for some months before making a decision to take up residence in the country. Nothing is quite the same as in first world countries, and expectations may not be met because of cultural differences or the considerable bureaucratic hurdles to cross. The important thing is not to burn one's bridges before moving to Honduras. We have met many people who enjoy life in Trujillo but others who feel trapped, as they now cannot afford to return to their native countries.

The people of Honduras are friendly and welcoming and need visitors to boost their economy with tourism dollars. They must have the help of first world countries in order to improve their productivity, feed themselves and their families, and pull themselves out of poverty. We love it in Honduras and believe that you would love it too.

Author with Jairo at his home near Trujillo

Noreen giving out blankets in Chiapas, Mexico

Chiapas Indians

Mayan Pyramid at Chichenitza

Noreen and Newton on Pat & Joska's Harley

Honduras

Tegucigalpa
*

*
Danli

NICARAGUA

* Leon

* Managua

* Granada

San Juan del Sur *

Costa Rica

U.S.A.

* Phoenix

El Paso

Nogales

Copper Canyon

* Durango

* San Blas
San Miguel *

Mexico City

Puerto Vallarta

Manzanillo

Taxco *

Zihautanejo

Oaxaca *

Acapulco

Puerto Escondido

Brownsville TX

Yucatan

Merida *

Chiapas

Guatemala

MEXICO

Chapter 8

Road Warriors of Central America

We have driven from Vancouver to Honduras and back twice now. And though it might sound daunting, it's an adventure that anyone can undertake. I must admit that before we tackled it the first time, we were a trifle apprehensive and talked to many people and consulted several books. Not one source gave us the full story, but we amalgamated the information and were confident that we could cope with almost any problem that might arise. After all, it wouldn't be an adventure if there were a possibility that *nothing* could go wrong.

Our First Drive

Our main reason driving down, apart from the adventure aspect, was to have a vehicle that we could use in the building of our house in Trujillo. It was also to transport sundry kitchen, electrical and other items, which are not readily available in Honduras. As we described in the previous chapter, the vehicle we selected was a 1985 Toyota 4 Runner, and the journey to Honduras was quite straightforward with only a few quirks.

We planned our journey through the United States using stopping places where there were Servas hosts. We stayed in Baker City, Oregon; Ogden, Utah; Grand Junction and Buena Vista, Colorado; Santa Fe and Bosque Farms, New Mexico; El Paso, San Antonio and Corpus Christi, Texas. Most days were full days of driving but we did break the journey to do some sightseeing. In Buena Vista we stayed on a ranch for two nights, and one day while there we tested our truck by crossing the continental divide twice at twelve thousand feet.

In New Mexico, we visited ancient Indian dwellings near Taos and the old parts of Santa Fe and Albuquerque. We were particularly impressed with the lovely adobe houses throughout the state. The mud houses were either left in their natural golden brown colour or painted white. The insides of the homes were always pleasantly cool by day and warm by night. The architectural designs were attractive both inside and out, the curves of the structures being very easy on the eye, making a relaxing environment.

After the ferry ride from Texas to Honduras (described in the previous chapter) the drive from the port of Puerto Cortez to Trujillo was an uneventful ride over good paved roads. From Trujillo, we continued south to Tegucigalpa over spectacular mountain roads and then to the Nicaragua border, just south of Danli.

Nicaragua

The border formalities were accomplished with the help of an agent who walked us through the complicated process of collecting stamps from all the officials who had them, and there were many. It is first necessary to cancel the Honduran vehicle stamp in your passport in order to leave the country yourself and this took us only a few minutes.

We spent most of the time on the Nicaraguan side, involved in finding the vehicle, engine and chassis numbers. I didn't even know we had a chassis number, but a man crawled under the truck and scraped away at mud and dirt and found one. They were most particular to take note of the accessories, such as radio and spare wheel, and they inspected the truck very carefully.

Everyone was most polite and the only hassle was finding a suitable agent from the hoard of men soliciting our business. I selected a quiet man from the back of the crowd and was well pleased with him, and in addition to his commission, he received a baseball hat from us. This was a big hit and he proudly wore it as he waved us good-bye to us when we entered Nicaragua.

We were first hit by the beauty of Nicaragua, by the excellent roads through green jungles and by the absence of traffic. Nicaragua had experienced civil war only a few years earlier and we had anticipated a feeling of tension in the country. In fact, we soon relaxed and felt very comfortable driving through and stopping in small towns on our route. As we neared Managua, the capital, the truck traffic increased and we took some quieter roads to avoid the congestion.

We found ourselves shopping for arts and crafts in Masaya and finally wound up in Granada where we checked in to the most imposing hotel right in the main square. It was full of North Americans enjoying a fine lifestyle at very low cost. Much of the town has been restored and there is little evidence remaining of the war.

The citizens are getting on with their lives, and with the help of the U.S.A., the economy seems to be booming.

Because we were not really comfortable with the idea of driving through Nicaragua, we had planned to pass through as quickly as possible. We soon realized that our discomfort was not warranted and wished we had allowed more time to spend in the country. After only one night in Nicaragua, we drove on down into Costa Rica.

Through Costa Rica and Back Again

We were not stopped once by any roadblocks for a papers check. There was no army presence and only normal police activity. Sometimes we came across a big green branch in the middle of the road and had to slow down to pass it. We soon realized that it was the Central American Highway Code signal for a hazard ahead. Usually it was a truck broken down or roadwork, but sometimes it was an accident or something more serious. It is a simple idea but nevertheless very effective

Northern Costa Rica is fairly flat and dry and after only cursory border checks, we drove south to see our teak plantation in Guanacaste. We were pleasantly surprised at the size of the trees and the extent of the plantation, even though it would be years before we would see any return on our investment.

We continued driving to the nation's capital, San Jose, where we looked up old friends and relived our expedition on horseback into the mountains some years earlier. We also looked up old friends in the Manuel Antonio National Park area and noticed how Costa Rica is developing with the huge influx of tourists they enjoy each year. The roads had been improved and travel around the country was much faster than on our first visit in 1989. We took advantage of our four-wheel drive truck to venture up infrequently travelled roads in the mountains.

There were coffee plantations where we saw only the occasional campesino, and we enjoyed extensive views over spectacular scenery. Christmas and New Year we spent with friends and visited beaches and rain-forests, swimming in the cool waters of both.

On our return trip north, we checked out the fancy resorts of Flamingo Beach and Tamarindo in the Guanacaste region and were pleased we had never tried to see them or stay there earlier. They are certainly beautiful and some places are quite exclusive. It didn't stop us from having a look around though; we simply flashed our "Hot Tours" business cards and were given the complete tour of facilities. We much preferred the cheaper, less sanitized places further south.

At the Costa Rican side of the border with Nicaragua, we spotted the Canadian flag on the packs of two hitchhikers and discovered they were from Vancouver. We offered them a ride across the long stretch of no-mans-land between the countries and suggested they come with us from Penas Blancas to San Juan del Sur. It was fun meeting the couple, Tim and Tina, who told us they worked in a hotel near Vancouver airport. We talked to them about Honduras and convinced them to come and visit us in Trujillo. This they did a few weeks later and we established a friendship that carried home to Vancouver where we met them again. On one occasion, Tina even helped us accommodate some Servas friends from Oregon, who were coming to Bali. We enjoy world-wide networking.

San Juan del Sur, Nicaragua, is an attractive place with a long curved beach on the Pacific. Travellers had recommended we check it out, and it certainly was a typical travellers' hangout. All the basic facilities were available including a bar for gringos and Europeans. The beach bars were quiet when we were there but we heard they became busy at weekends with people from the capital, Managua. Even during mid-week, the town felt alive and I felt it had the character and beauty to become a popular resort as tourism develops in Nicaragua.

Managua is less than two hours drive north of San Juan del Sur and we had decided not to stay there as there had been reports that it was dangerous for tourists. Instead we drove into the city looking for the centre but never found it. The city was devastated in 1972 by a major earthquake that killed over 18,000 people, and it suffered damage during the revolution in 1978--79. Managua has never been rebuilt and the scene in the city is reminiscent of bomb damage after the war in Europe, making driving there eerie.

We drove on past volcanoes to the old capital of Leon, which boasts Central America's largest cathedral. It is a lovely colonial city but has again suffered from the revolution and a major volcanic eruption in 1992. There is still evidence of the revolution in the form of graffiti on walls in the centre of Leon but a monument for reconciliation is also very prominent next to the cathedral.

After just one night, we headed for the border with Honduras in our truck with the license plate from British Columbia. There were the usual formalities and delays at the border on both sides, and we were getting a bit frazzled in the midday heat.

The final clearance was with the drug squad in Honduras. They spotted our British Columbia plates and thought, as we were heading north, that we must be from Columbia. They started to give us the once-over using six men in black uniforms armed with AK 47 machine guns and accompanied by dogs. We opened the back of the truck to allow them to search and they immediately found Noreen's bottle of rum. They thought that it was a present for them and held it up while Noreen told them to put it back at once--it was *hers*. Next they moved to the front of the car and asked me to take off the door panels, which had obviously not been removed since the car was built.

This was too much for me and I started shouting in English that we were not from Columbia, we were from Canada and we had no drugs or arms with us. Luckily I had chosen the right moment and they were so taken aback that they stepped away and waved us on. I think that the armed soldiers may have intimidated some people, but we had been stopped so often by roadblocks, had nothing to hide and were confident we could get away with verbally abusing the menacing men.

Previous chapters recount and here I will continue describing our time in Honduras from the Honduran border with Guatemala at Aqua Calientes. It is a busy truck stop and the piles of paper work are tedious and time consuming on the Honduran side but easy on the Guatemalan side.

Guatemala

We drove the route from the border to Antigua. We had taken this route by bus some years previously, but this time it was much faster and more comfortable. We had hoped to avoid the infamous Guatemala City but there seems to be no way around it so there we were, late on a Sunday afternoon, in a very poor part of the city, when our trusty Toyota decided to go no further.

We pulled off the road into a closed gas station and stared helplessly at the inert but hot engine, hoping that as it cooled, it might become re-energized. Indeed, after fifteen minutes or so, during which several curious bystanders had come to offer advice in Spanish, we were able to restart the engine and proceeded for about five minutes before it died again.

We pulled into a side street off the busy highway and immediately regretted it, as we were in an even worse area and darkness could only be an hour away. If we had to leave the car there overnight, would there be anything left in the morning? I sat and pondered the engine problem and decided it had to be a fuel failure. I listened and heard a faint hissing from a hose and secured it with a hair-grip. That was all it took and the engine roared to life and stayed alive until we reached Antigua as night fell.

We found a lovely hotel that not only had a garden courtyard but also a fireplace in the bedroom; it was close to the centre of the city and its price was reasonable. It was great to revisit Antigua and we spent a day seeing places we had discovered on our first visit during Semana Santa a few years earlier.

We shopped a little and drove on to Panajachel where we shopped some more. We had to take advantage of the space in our truck to convey some of those gorgeous weavings back to Vancouver.

That night, we reached Huehuetenango in northern Guatemala. It is a centre of coffee growing and there are warehouses full of sacks of beans on all the city approaches. We stopped at some, hoping to buy some beans to take home, but were disappointed not to find any roasted whole beans. It reminded me of "Water, water everywhere"-- but not a "drop to drink." In the morning we drove into the mountains on unpaved trails enjoying the scenery of rolling hills. We came across a school and surprised teachers and pupils when we stopped to give them maps and supplies that we had left over from those we had brought down for our adopted Honduran school. We saw no other vehicles, just pedestrians and horses.

Mexico

We continued to the Mexican border at La Mesilla through a deep, winding canyon and past tiny Indian villages where they wore their traditional, colourful costumes. At the border, an official wanted us to return to Guatemala City for a transit visa but after some pleading, and with the assistance of another, more sympathetic official, we were allowed through but only given a visa for two weeks. We turned south for a while until we reached the Pan American Highway, which parallels the west coast of Mexico and the Sierra Madre de Chiapas; then headed north-west towards Salina Cruz.

On the first afternoon, in the state of Chiapas, we were stopped no less than six times by army roadblocks. Chiapas is renowned for its independence movement by disgruntled Chiapas Indians, and there had been recent outbreaks of fighting in the area, so tensions were running high. Soldiers at the checkpoints were all most civil, some were scared, and all were young.

Throughout the length of Mexico we were stopped on a further fourteen occasions. Sometimes we had to drive over a pit where anti-drug smuggling enforcers would prod away with a screwdriver at our undercarriage looking for contraband. At other blocks we would simply be stopped for a chat to see where we had been and where we were going. Not once were we asked for a bribe--or maybe we just didn't understand their Spanish.

We worked our way along the coast and stayed first in Puerto Escondido, which is accustomed to tourists and caters for them well. Mariachi bands entertained us as we dined by candlelight at a beachside restaurant. Continuing along, we came to Acapulco, which I had visited in 1969 and I really noticed major changes. It is now a huge city with scores of high-rise hotels lining beaches teaming with millions of tourists on their packaged holidays. I couldn't think of a worse place to go to be swallowed by the seething hordes.

The only good memory I have of Acapulco is seeing my first new Beetle. A huge transporter truck had twenty brightly coloured Volkswagen Beetles with their complementary coloured fenders.

Quickly we drove on to Zihuatanejo where Noreen had been some years earlier. Again the place was hardly recognizable to her and she had trouble showing me around. The old town has been developed and a new one built just north of it called Ixtapa, which is exclusively for tourists. Apart from some traditional architecture, he flavour of Mexico has been nicely killed.

We hurried on to Manzanillo, which remains a grubby little town catering for business and commercial interests more than for tourism, it seems. There was a strip of development north of the town, which was quite attractive but our destination was the village of Santiago. We stayed in a lovely condominium apartment belonging to Bill and Judy, friends in Vancouver, and became normal holidaymakers for a couple of days. We swam in the pool and in the sea, walked the beach, and dined in fine restaurants while we watched dramatic sunsets. We would have stayed longer, but our visa was running out and we had no more time to laze around.

We stopped at Club Med just north of Santiago, but I was unable to talk my way in there, even though I had spent a bachelor's holiday there some years ago. The drive north to Puerto Vallarta was a far cry from the previous time I had made it; the road is paved and goes fast through lovely countryside. Puerto Vallarta used to be such a fine traditional, sleepy Mexican seaside town when I first visited it in 1973 but now it, too, has developed beyond recognition. We couldn't even find anywhere to park the truck. That was all right, though, as

I didn't need to see the new Vallarta. Instead we made our way up to San Blas for the night. It is a sleepy little village where overgrown hippies still stay. We liked it enough to make a point of heading there on our next trip through Mexico.

The rest of the trip up the coast past, Mazatlan, Los Mochis and Guaymas, was pretty boring apart from the thousands of mango trees in full fruit. We saw truck loads being sent to markets around the world. It is a favourite fruit of ours and we gorged ourselves as often as we could. After a night in Hermosillo, a pleasant enough town in the industrial north, we drove to Nogales, the border with the United States.

The Excited States

After spending six months in Central America, we were a little nervous crossing the border with our truck-full of goods, but we need not have worried at all. On leaving the Mexican side of the border, I had to run back from no-man's-land to the customs station to turn in my tourist windshield sticker. I never did turn in our visitor permits but it didn't appear to matter. Border officials were very casual. On the United States side, we were just asked how long we had been in Mexico and we honestly answered two weeks, not mentioning we had also visited Costa Rica, Nicaragua and Honduras. It is always wise to answer questions from customs officers directly with no elaboration.

We had been unable to purchase insurance for our vehicle in Central America or in Mexico and had not been too concerned. The U.S.A. was another matter, and we did not wish to take any risks in that litigious country. There were no agencies at the border or along the route north until we reached Tucson, but we found an "All State" office in a shopping centre and asked to be insured. We thought it would be easy, but not so. We had to have a U.S. address and came up with a Servas host address--another advantage of belonging to that wonderful organization.

Our Servas hosts in South Tempe had been our hosts in Albuquerque six months earlier. We had become friends with them and when they moved to Arizona they invited us to stay in their new home. We stayed a couple of nights and took the opportunity of visiting friends in beautiful, pristine Scottsdale. We were struck by the affluence of the entire Phoenix area, especially the elaborate homes with fabulous cactus gardens in Scottsdale. Such a contrast from the third world countries we had been visiting for the previous six months. It was a real culture shock for us. Since we were so near the Grand Canyon, we decided to detour to see this natural marvel again. It really is stupendous. It is too bad that so many people want to see it!

It was the same in Bryce Canyon National Park-- thousands of sightseers, even in April when it is still cold and snow remains on the ground. We had a little scare while driving towards Bryce canyon: as we rounded a curve in the road, we came face to face with an aeroplane which had just landed on the road in front of us. We took immediate evasive action and swung off the road to avoid the plane wings, which would have clipped our roof rack. Luckily the big bus behind us had time to stop just before the plane turned sharply into a field. Apparently one of the sightseeing aircraft had experienced problems that necessitated an emergency landing on the highway.

We rejoined the route we had taken south at Salt Lake City, Utah, continued to Ogden where some Servas friends lived, and then drove to Baker City, Oregon. On this trip we made time to check out the Oregon Trail Visitor Centre. Videos and dioramas with the voices of those trying to make a new life in the Wild West provide a dramatic portrayal of the tough life of the first pioneers. The trail actually ran through the ranch that was the home of another Servas host, and we felt privileged to be so close to the history of the development of a nation. We were now within striking distance of our home in Vancouver and sped back without further delay. It is always nice to be back home, even when you have had an adventurous six months in six countries, enjoying the warmth and sunshine of the tropics, while your friends have been suffering the cold and wet of the Pacific North West.

Chapter 9

On the Road Again....

Our Second Drive

Our next trip south to Central America was just after Hurricane Mitch struck and, with our truckload of relief supplies, we set out to drive down. In readiness for possible border hassles, we had checked with the various consulates in Vancouver. Mexico required a transit visa, which was free and took one day to get. Guatemala required a notarized packing list of all our goods, authenticated by the Notary Society of British Columbia, and those in turn authenticated by the Guatemalan Consul.

In the event, we had a lawyer notarize the list for no fee, but he had to be authenticated by the Law Society. It took a lot of running around and the Law Society wanted to charge us an exorbitant fee for their stamp. We felt this was totally unnecessary and immoral for a list of donated goods and refused to pay, leaving with an unauthenticated document but lots of lovely gold seals and red stickers. Honduras advised us we would need no documentation.

In fact, Mexican authorities stopped us south of Nogales and told us we shouldn't have crossed at that border and that we had to return to the United States and recross in El Paso or Brownsville with a whole bunch of paper work. I explained that we were on a mission of mercy and showed them our beautifully sealed packing list. Finally, when they realized I had no intention of returning to the U.S.A., they let us proceed.

At the Guatemalan border we were waved through and didn't have a chance of showing them the documents we had specially prepared for them. The Honduran customs were awkward as usual and demanded a packing list, which we had fortunately prepared for Guatemala, and they let us in after a payment of duty--for goods donated to their country no less. Don't ever underestimate the stupidity of border officials.

The drive down through the United States was on a completely different route from our first trip. We made time to visit several friends on the way in Eugene, Oregon; San Francisco, California; and Scottsdale and Tempe, Arizona. In Mexico we retraced our route down the west coast to San Blas and to Santiago where we delivered a set of soccer uniforms to the local barber for the town team. A group in Vancouver had donated the uniforms and we smuggled them into Mexico.

We then drove north-east to Lake Chapala and the town of Ajijic, which is a favourite retirement haven for ex-patriot Americans. It is not a very exciting town, and the lake is receding at an alarming rate and is not suitable for swimming. The climate is most agreeable though. The gringos all eat out early and go to bed at about eight o'clock. Friends who had lived there some years earlier had moved further east to San Miguel de Allende, our next destination.

We took a rough road around Lake Chapala past poor villages, which contrasted alarmingly with the homes of the rich Americans in Ajijic. In one village we took a wrong turn and wound up asking for directions. A group of people--all wanting to know what we were selling from our truck--surrounded us.

San Miguel de Allende is a glorious Spanish colonial town set on a hillside. It is known for its art schools and is popular with ex-patriots for its culture, architecture and climate. We were guests of a friend, Robert, who had been on a Hot Tours trip to Bali. He was eighty six years old and walked us off our feet as he guided us around the city, showing us nooks and crannies we would never have found on our own.

Robert had spent some of his youth riding the trains across the United States as a hobo. He had even lived in Central Park, New York, for a time. He had lied about his age when he wanted to come to Bali with us, as he thought we might not take him. In fact, he was less trouble than anyone on the trip as he had boundless energy and a great personality to go with his stories. At home in British Columbia, he helps his artist wife, Francis, create huge murals on the sides of buildings. His job is to clamber over scaffolding--at age eight-six!

One evening in San Miguel, we attended a poetry reading in English; it was organized by the local community, which was not something we had expected. We took our leave from Robert and his wife and drove to

Taxco, the silver capital of Mexico, where we spent two nights. During the day we walked the steep hillsides and explored the scores of silver shops and market stalls. There were bargains to be had everywhere and we bought items at wholesale prices. Nightlife was active with political rallies going on each night. The party banners in the square on the first night were replaced by the opponent party's banners the following night. The same people attended and the same bands played. We watched it all from restaurant balconies overlooking the main square.

Oaxaca was our next stop but the city did not appeal to us. We did visit some interesting Mayan ruins south of town, but the Spanish invaders had desecrated these. The Catholics had raised the Mayan structures and erected a church using the stones carved by the Indians.

We carried on to Tehuantepec, a stop on the Pan American Highway, and headed directly into the heart of Chiapas, the rebel State. We had heard of numerous bandits working the highways in recent years, but there had been no major incidents in recent months. The roads were quiet and the hills severe. We passed through spectacular mountain scenery and small Indian villages perched on the mountainsides. The villagers were not keen on having their photographs taken.

Our trusty Toyota was not too keen on the hills, and she overheated, stopping at the most inconvenient location in the centre of rebel country. After a cooling off period, she allowed us to drive on but decided to stop several times more. We sought the help of a mechanic in a small town who suggested we needed parts that were only available from Mexico City. We limped on and, as the day grew older, we climbed still further until eventually we reached 8,000 feet and the city of San Cristobal de Las Casas.

The city was a wonderful surprise to us. The elevation keeps it cool by night and warm by day. The old colonial haciendas are now beautiful hotels and very reasonably priced. There are delicatessens, Internet cafes, shops and restaurants all around the central area and scores of European tourists. Americans have all been scared away by their State Department warnings of violence in the area. They seem to overreact to problems and leave their warnings in effect long after peace has broken out.

We loved the city of San Cristobal and felt completely safe at all times. We did buy dolls and photos of the rebel leader, Marcos, dressed in his guerrilla uniform and mask. I inserted one of the photos of Marcos and some of his rebels in my album amongst the ones I had taken of our trip--and this either worried or impressed our friends at home. Chiapas is not a scary place and we returned there on our next trip north.

We crossed into Guatemala at La Mesilla where we had crossed going north nine months earlier. Because we were on familiar territory, we were very nonchalant about the border formalities and walked through the process with ease. The drive to the border through Chiapas that morning was mainly downhill and our trusty Toyota had no complaints. But, as we started to climb through the long canyon to the Highlands of Guatemala, the truck did begin to complain. She stopped several times and I thought we were being very kind to her in the heat of the midday sun by letting her rest under a tree every hour.

We were in the middle of nowhere on the top of a mountain when she decided to boil over her radiator. Out of nowhere came some children, and Noreen followed them to a tiny mud hut. A peasant lady provided her with a pail of water for us to give the truck.

On another occasion, a trucker had stopped to see if he could be of any assistance. Everybody we came across was most friendly and helpful, and we had no thoughts of all the evil things we had heard about attacks on tourists in Guatemala. Finally I thought some more about the overheating problem and decided to change gears manually rather than letting the automatic transmission do it for us. That did the trick and the truck behaved itself for the rest of our trip.

The delays of the day caused us to be two hours behind schedule, and this left us on the highway between major towns. We did not want to risk stopping in one of the villages en route as there would be very basic accommodation and nowhere secure to leave the truck overnight. We had to push on to Antigua, even though darkness had fallen and we had vowed never to drive at night in Central America.

The Pan American Highway was quite busy with trucks and we felt relatively safe continuing to drive, but the absence of road signs made us nervous. It seemed to take forever to reach the turn-off for Antigua. We pulled in at the same hotel in which we had stayed on our trip north and collapsed into bed after a very long hot day. Unfortunately, the hotel was not as quiet as it had been nine months earlier, for the road had been repaved and was now a main thoroughfare. We had not noticed the change when we checked in after dark. This is another reason why one should never drive at night and leave enough daylight hours to check out any new environment. Antigua once again enthralled us and we felt comfortable to be back for the third time.

We had breakfast at Dona Luis's as usual and enjoyed her wonderful coffee with a huge bowl of granola and fruit liberally coated with syrup. We are real stick-in-the-muds when we find places we like, and we return to the same places to eat the same things.

The last leg of our journey took us all the way from Antigua, through Guatemala City, Chiquimula and Esquipulas to the border with Honduras at Aqua Calientes. Oh, how we hate that border crossing. That is where we were unduly delayed and had to pay duty on the donated goods we were bringing in for victims of Mitch.

We reached San Pedro Sula before dark and settled in at a small central hotel. In the morning we had a major shopping spree at a huge new centre, which carried all kinds of North American goods and foods that we knew would not be available to us in Trujillo. We carried on to La Ceiba for an overnight stay with friends and arrived in Trujillo early the following morning.

Customs Hoops

This chapter, about driving a vehicle to Central America, would not be complete without details of the hoops through which you have to jump when you leave a country without your vehicle. We had thought we would sell the truck in Honduras, as, after Mitch, there was little point in building a house for ourselves and we would have no need of a big truck.

Our plan had been to build a house and rent it out while we were not there. Without tourists there would be no rental market and we could not afford to leave the house empty.

The customs, or *Aduana*, advised us that the duty on our fifteen-year-old truck would be three thousand dollars. This would make it prohibitively expensive for any buyer, so we had the choice of driving the truck back to Vancouver or leaving it in bond at customs. We chose the latter and the *Aduana* at Puerto Castilla, near Trujillo said they would take care of the truck outside their office for ten months until we returned the following year. There would be no storage charges and when we returned, we could apply for a permit to keep the truck in the country for a further two months.

That all sounded very fair and the chief of *Aduana* was most co-operative. We left Honduras by air for England and were happy that our truck would be secure until we returned. Then the chief of *Aduana* in Puerto Castilla was replaced.

The new chief had a totally different perspective on the situation. He advised our friends in Trujillo that the truck was in Honduras illegally and that the duty should be paid or the truck should be removed from the country. In addition, a fine was imposed for keeping the truck in the country contrary to our original permit. Our pleas to have the original agreement honoured were ignored - even though we had a receipt for the truck stamped in Noreen's passport.

We asked some of our friends to telephone Aduana for us and even the Bishop of Trujillo telephoned on our behalf--after all, the name of the customs chief was "Jesus." Several times, *Aduana* threatened to sell the truck to cover their "costs." At another time they said that we owed a fine, storage charges and duty, and that we had to remove the truck from the country.

We hired a well-known lawyer in Tegucigalpa to act on our behalf but even that was a hassle. To give her power of attorney, we had to have it drawn up in Spanish and English, have it notarized, authenticated by the Notary Society of British Columbia, authenticated by the Honduran Consul in Vancouver, and then sent by courier to Honduras. All this cost time and lots of money.

The lawyer went to work with the retainer we gave her and finally obtained an agreement for a fine and storage fee to be paid. The truck would also have to be removed from the country for seventy-two hours. She arranged for a total stranger to drive the vehicle out of Honduras and into Guatemala for three days and to pay the stranger five days wages--plus expenses. We turned this idea down and found someone we knew and trusted who would do the job for us. They contacted a "friend" within the *Aduana* office and delayed the process for a few more weeks.

Meanwhile we were in Indonesia, leading a Hot Tours group to Bali and Lombok, and in the group was a lady from Trujillo. We told her our tale of woe, and she suggested we contact a writer for *Honduras this Week*, the English language newspaper of Honduras; the writer had legal training in the U.S.A. and Honduras. We e-mailed her from Bali and she immediately took up our cause without payment of any retainer. Within days she had spoken to some senior people in *Aduana* in Tegucigalpa and obtained an agreement simply to remove the truck to Guatemala for three days; she also arranged for the payment of a nominal amount for storage but no fine.

We again spoke to the friend who would drive the vehicle for us and, because it was near Christmas, he obtained a further delay and suggested we come down to Honduras in January and drive the truck out ourselves.

We flew to Trujillo in January and went straight to the *Aduana* office in Puerto Castilla to meet the new chief. He spoke no English but could tell we were pretty angry about the whole deal. His boss had said there would be no fine, and now we had to negotiate a storage fee. The body levying the fee was the Port Authority so we went from office to office until we met the head of the Port. He agreed that there should be no fee at all, since we were helping the poor of Honduras. The only thing left to do was to get the truck going again and drive it to Guatemala. The *Aduana* officials wouldn't let us take the truck to Trujillo for an oil change or repairs to the fuel system, so we had to get a mechanic to do the work outside the *Aduana* office.

The day came to leave and an armed policeman was assigned to escort us to the border--I am not sure why, but perhaps they thought we would sell the car or break it into parts. The policeman, Oscar, had a wad of papers for the car, and as we passed various checkpoints on the road to the border, we were waved through without any hindrance. Oscar spoke no English at all and spent most of the time sleeping. When we stopped for a break, he stood on guard by the truck--clearly he took his job seriously.

At the border with Guatemala at Aqua Calientes, Oscar took the papers into the office and after twenty minutes, re-emerged and called us into the office. Noreen and I were ushered into a bare interrogation room with two men, one of whom spoke perfect English. They told us that we had a problem; our papers were not correct and that we had to pay them a fine and return to Puerto Castilla. I told them that I did not have a problem but they did, as we had been told our papers were in order, and we had no intention of paying a fine or driving for nine hours back to Puerto Castilla.

They saw that I was becoming really angry and moved us into the comfortable office of the manager, who was away in Tegucigalpa meeting his boss. The boss was the same man who had agreed with our lady from the press that we could leave the country with no fine. They tried to telephone both Tegucigalpa and Puerto Castilla, but it was then around four o'clock in the afternoon and no one was answering their phones. They told us we would have to leave our truck with them, go into the neighbouring town of Nueva Ocotepeque to spend the night and return in the morning. I told them that I had no intention of leaving the car with them, that it was our car and they were not going to steal it from us. I would call my lawyer and the Canadian Embassy if necessary.

They backed down a little at that but told us we would be in trouble if we were stopped by the police and had no papers. We pointed out that we had an armed policeman with us and "Where could we go anyway?" They finally agreed and we checked into our hotel with Oscar. We gave Oscar some money for dinner but he stayed with the truck until it was parked in a secure parking area and didn't leave until he had arranged for a pick-up truck to be parked behind us so we couldn't get away, even if we had wanted to.

In the morning, we drove back to the border and presented ourselves at the manager's office. He had returned from Tegucigalpa and spoken with his boss there that morning after learning about the two Canadians who were causing a big disturbance. He came out of his office and shook our hands, smiling. He told us that there was no problem that could not be handled in his office and that the necessary paperwork would be prepared in an hour or two. His assistant then told us that an agency would have to prepare exportation documents and "Would a fee of seven hundred *lempira* (forty-six dollars) be alright?" We pondered for half a second and agreed; it could have been far, far worse.

The paperwork was prepared, and as we were leaving, the customs manager said we did not have to leave the country for seventy-two hours after all; we could return to Honduras that same day if we wished. After all the trouble we had been given, we didn't wish and we decided to go on to Antigua for a relaxing weekend. Oscar came with us to see that we checked in to Guatemala and only when the gate came down behind us did he relax and wave good-bye. He was not a happy man as he had hoped to spend the night having fun in San Pedro Sula instead of vegetating in the dull town of Nueva Ocotepeque.

We were pleased to have the saga of *Aduana* and our truck behind us, and we enjoyed our three days in Antigua. We also decided that we would not return to Honduras through Agua Calientes but would try the small border crossing at El Florido, near Copan Ruinas. This was a wise decision.

The road to the border on the Guatemalan side was under construction but mostly newly paved and we made excellent time through gorgeous countryside. The border post was a simple collection of huts and the officials were very relaxed and helpful. There was no need for an agent to help, and the officials filled in all the forms for you. The inspection was only momentary, and we were on our way back into Honduras, legally again for three months.

As far as costs were concerned, we were lucky that we got off so lightly with the *Aduana*. We have heard other horror stories from ex-patriots who have had to pay horrendous fines and storage charges, especially in Puerto Cortez. In one case, we saw a missionary in Puerto Cortez being held there for days. He had a bus full of donations for an orphanage in Honduras and the *Aduana* wanted to charge him three thousand dollars duty on the used clothes and other goods. It does pay to fight the bureaucracy, but you have to have lots of time and be prepared to take the problems to higher and higher levels.

La Routa Maya--Honduras, Guatemala, Belize and Mexico

That was a long digression from our travels in Central America but does indicate one of the things that you can encounter. We decided not to keep our truck in Honduras, or to try to sell it there, and drove it back to Vancouver taking in Tikal, Guatemala, Belize (the old British Honduras), the Yucatan Peninsula of Mexico, Chiapas again, and thence through Mexico and the States to Vancouver. We took two days to reach Tikal, stopping in the small beach town of Omoa, Honduras. There we ran into several people with whom we shared mutual friends in Trujillo and we were able to update them on the latest gossip and scandals there. They were able to fill us in with past events in Trujillo, which were not talked about by the present residents.

We drove into Guatemala over rough roads and through five rivers, all of which required four-wheel drive, and we noted the contrast between the roads of Guatemala and Honduras. Those in Guatemala are beautifully built and paved all the way to Tikal. We broke the journey in Rio Dulce, where we ran into an old drug-dealing friend from Trujillo who had changed his name to escape the law and an irate husband of his wild girlfriend. He showed us a great waterfront hotel on the called Bruno's, where we swam in the pool and watched the "yachties" do their thing with their expensive boats. I can never understand how these people do so little with so much money.

Tikal is a magnificent Mayan City set in the Peten jungles. We reached the park as the gates were opened in the morning. There was only a trickle of tourists as we entered and walked under the jungle canopy to the grand square of the city. The square is surrounded by enormous stone structures which just beg to be climbed. We climbed them to obtain great photographs and videos in the early morning light. The sun was rising over the pyramids, which were almost obscured in the jungle by the tentacles of vines and rapid-growing undergrowth.

If one is squeamish about heights, it is not the place to go, as the steps on the pyramids are steep and guard rails are nonexistent. American insurance companies would have a liability fit if they were asked to insure people who climbed the pyramids. The views, peace and tranquillity of the area were awesome. We were lucky to see scores of parrots, butterflies and cotamundi as we walked several miles through the jungle and around the pyramids and other structures. Some of the structures are in their original state of ruin, others under various stages of reconstruction and restoration. As we left the park, the busloads of tourists were arriving and starting to shatter the peace of this magical place.

The Belize border is not far from Tikal and we cleared the border formalities with little effort. Belize, being formally called British Honduras, is naturally English speaking although it is hard to tell if you listen to locals talking amongst themselves. Their musical speech is similar to the West Indian lilt with Spanish and ancient English thrown in.

It is necessary to buy liability insurance for vehicles brought into the country, unlike other Central American countries and Mexico, so we did so for the first time on our trip. Initially the drive through Belize was pretty, with picturesque rivers and green trees. This soon deteriorated to absolutely boring semidesert country, and we sped on for endless miles until we reached Belmopan, the new capital city of Belize.

We had read about the reluctance of the populace to accept the new capital after having Belize City the capital for so long but nothing prepared us for what we found, or didn't find, in Belmopan. Certainly, the country of Belize is small, but Belmopan is a tiny capital with almost nothing in the way of shops or other commercial activity. We drove completely around the place looking for the centre, which apparently doesn't exist. There were some government buildings but these were deserted, as it was a Sunday. We gather that many government workers still live near Belize City and commute to work a few days a week.

Continuing along the main highway to the old capital, we entered civilization and made our way through the poor, black-populated areas of the waterfront. It was quite colourful and had shades of former colonial influence and had become rather run-down. The centre of the city was busy, even on a Sunday, and with its lovely old buildings, some beautifully restored; it was in far better shape than the new capital.

We had been warned that Belize City was a dangerous place and that violent crime and burglaries were common, so we had decided not to stay there. On reflection, I would have liked to have lingered and explored the city further, but we had to carry on until we found a place in Orange Walk. On the way, we passed the body of a woman who had been killed as she crossed the road after alighting from a bus. That accident could have involved us, had we been a few minutes earlier, and we realized how important that insurance could have been.

Orange Walk has little to offer and the only hotels both had discos attached, so a peaceful night was not going to be possible. Dinner was available only from one of the Chinese restaurants. The one we chose had only Chinese speaking staff and they couldn't even read their own menu! We had to enlist the aid of a local, slightly drunk Indian to translate from English to Belize English and then to Chinese!

Perhaps we shall return to Belize one day, but it will only be to have a quick look at Belize City and to visit the Cayes, which form part of the second longest barrier reef in the world. We have seen the other end of the reef in Roatan, Honduras, and visited the longest reef, the Great Barrier Reef of Australia, so it may be some time before we see the Belize Cayes. Once you have dived in the Banda Islands of Indonesia, it is hard to get excited about other dive sites.

The lands of the Mayan people extend from Honduras and Guatemala through Belize to the Yucatan Peninsula of Mexico. We continued on La Ruta Maya from Belize towards the most visited Mayan site at Chichen Itza.

On the way, we stopped at Playa del Carmen, the popular tourist spot on the Caribbean side of the Yucatan. The main attraction is the unbelievably turquoise sea and fine white sand on the beaches in the area. We actually tried to stay south of Playa del Carmen at Tulum, but there was no bank from which to obtain credit card cash advances, and the hotels do not accept cards either, so we had to press on.

Tulum looked pretty quiet and laid back, but Playa del Carmen was a zoo of tourists and restaurants, and full of tacky shops. Nevertheless, we stayed a couple of days to relax at the beach and to enjoy some typical Mexican cuisine. We also took a quick boat trip to Cozumel. This is a place to be avoided if at all possible, due to the number of tacky tourists and cruise-ship passengers who besiege the town and shops to buy duty-free goods at inflated prices. Cozumel is not Mexico; neither is Cancun.

Cancun is an amazing stretch of fancy hotels attracted by the Mexican government to encourage massive tourism development. The development takes advantage of the natural resource of beautiful beaches and the Caribbean Sea. If you want to veg-out in luxury, this is the place for you but don't pretend you are in Mexico, because you are in a huge international resort where Spanish is a minority language.

There are two routes to Chichen Itza, the fast, expensive toll highway and the slower, more interesting roads that take you through scores of villages and over even more scores of speed bumps. We took the slower route and thanked our Toyota for putting up with the annoying *topes*. Many of these horrible bumps are not posted and some of them are designed to stop one completely.

The ruins in Chichen Itza are impressive but they were overrun with crowds of people when we were there. It was at that point that Noreen announced that she didn't want to visit any more "piles of old rocks" covered with people, unless they were in Egypt.

We carried on to Merida, which is a beautiful, old Spanish colonial city. It is a vibrant place full of activity and energy. We walked around the central areas a lot, enjoying the Spanish and other European architecture that graces the wide streets and boulevards. Merida was developed as a centre for the production and shipment of sisal. This name was passed to Sisal, the port nearby. Much of the trade was directly with Europe, hence the influence on the architecture of the city. Apparently, now it is a good place for face-lifts and liposuction.

The Other Mexico

The next destination for us was San Cristobal de Las Casas in Chiapas. We took two days to make the journey in the sweltering Yucatan heat during which our truck balked at the 106F (41C) degree temperatures. We completed the final assault on the dizzy heights of the mountains of Chiapas in the early morning and entered San Cristobal whose temperature was a chilly 50F (10C) degrees.

I spoke about this lovely city before and our opinion of it has not changed. Often it is not a good idea to revisit a place you liked a lot the first time in case it does not live up to the rosy memories, but in this, case we were not disappointed and would go back again given the chance. The surrounding villages we visited were quite poor but nothing like the poverty we have seen in Honduras. The agitators in the Zapatista movement have obviously had some effect, and there is still an undercurrent of anxiety by the Mexican Government, which manifests itself with increased military presence and frequent roadblocks.

We had some blankets to donate to some of the poor, cold Indians in the mountains but were advised not to distribute them ourselves. It could be construed as being a political action, and we could have been run out of the country. This was the advice of a human rights group and they could have been overreacting, but we accepted their recommendation. We did see one poor old lady with her child and gave her a blanket directly. It was near the village of San Juan Chamula where the most bizarre things occur. In the main square is the usual church but the inside is far from usual.

To enter the church, you first have to find the tourist office to buy a permit and agree not to take photographs inside. The floor of the church is strewn with pine needles and statues of saints surround the perimeter in glass cages. There are no pews or chairs, and individual worshippers set up their own areas where they burn groups of candles and mutter strange prayers in their native Indian language. Spanish is not spoken in the town and Catholicism is not practised in the cathedral. Photography of the inside of the church and of people is not permitted, and signs at the entrance to town tell you this. Small children are the exception, however, and many offer to pose for photos for a few pesos.

We left the town with only a few photographs but with the strong memory of a people still practising their original pagan rituals, modified by the colonialist priests from Spain. We have committed the scenery of the area to long term memory, as the panorama is too vast to be captured on film or video.

The long descent to the new capital of Chiapas, Tuxtla Guiterrez, winds through numerous s-bends and villages with colourful inhabitants; there are dramatic views and picturesque sights at every turn. Sightseeing is a little hard to do when I am driving, but somehow I manage, while Noreen keeps her eyes on the road for me.

We retraced our steps, taken two years earlier, and paused for breaks in Puerto Escondido, Zihuatanejo and Santiago, even staying in the same places and eating in some of the same restaurants. All along our route on the main roads, we were stopped at army roadblocks. This is particularly annoying and sometimes they ask to see car papers or passports, and at other times they ask where we are going. When Noreen asked them once why we were being stopped, they replied it was because of security. She then asked them why they were afraid of us. Only once, in more than a score of stops, was the car even cursorily searched.

People ask us if we feel safe in Central America and we answer "Yes, safer than in the U.S.A. or in Mexico." Who can really feel safe with so many young soldiers brandishing automatic weapons at every turn in the road? Mexico is still far from a free democratic state and very much a third world country--something many tourists don't realize, unless they drive out of the sanitized tourist zones.

Yorkshire Dales, England

United Kingdom

Skye

Aberdeen*

Scotland

Glasgow
*

Edinburgh

Northern
Ireland

Belfast *

Lake
District

Dales

Liverpool

England

Angelsey

Nottingham

*Dolgllau

Norwich*

Cambridge*

Wales

Newport
*

Oxford*

London
*

Cornwall

Devon

Northern Ireland

Enniskillen
*

Sligo
*

Clifden *

Galway
*

* Dublin

Cliffs of Moher *

Waterford
*

Dingle *

Cork
*

Rosslare
*

Ring of
Kerry *

Kinsale *

IRELAND

Chapter 10

Land of Brits and Paddys

I have seen more of the British Isles since I moved to Canada, thirty-six years ago, than I did in my first twenty-four years as a resident of the United Kingdom. I was born in what was Newport, Monmouthshire, England, but in the seventies there was a reorganization of the counties and some re-naming, which left Newport in Gwent, Wales. Now I don't know whether I am English or Welsh. I have relatives from both England and Wales and I feel I can switch allegiance whenever it suits me. This is particularly important when I visit Ireland where the Welsh are more readily accepted than the English who were the common enemy from time to time. Anyway, we are both Celtic.

On our many visits to the United Kingdom of Great Britain and Northern Ireland, we have explored most corners of "The Sceptred Isle." I love Britain dearly, but only to visit, and not to live in permanently again. I think it is mainly the weather that gets me down. It is never stable for long and it is difficult to organize events that are dependent on fine weather.

This chapter is an amalgamation of our visits and will highlight the most interesting places from my perspective. It may help people decide which places to visit whether they live in the United Kingdom or in North America. Sometimes it takes a resident to leave and then return before he gets a true picture of a country.

Wales and Monmouthshire

Naturally I should start with my home county of Monmouthshire, which was created from the Lordship Marchers in the sixteenth century. Previously it was a kind of buffer zone between England and Wales but it was listed as one of the English counties. Acts of Parliament always applied to Wales and Monmouthshire and the most significant alliance with Wales was when it was decreed that pubs be closed on Sundays. It was said that there was more beer drunk in Wales and Monmouthshire on Sunday than in the whole of England for an entire week.

Newport Rugby Club was always affiliated with the Welsh Rugby Union but also to the English Rugby Union, and in the past, players from Newport have played on opposite sides in International matches.

The seat of the Archbishop of Wales was in my own Cathedral Church of St. Woollos when I was a chorister there. This is to show that my singing comes from an honest background, although it has been much modified by the various rugby clubs I have joined from time to time. It doesn't matter if Monmouthshire is English or Welsh; it is still a very beautiful county with wide variations in topography from west to east.

The Western Valleys have the typical Welsh mining communities spread along the valley bottoms with the remains of the old coal slag heaps scarring the hillsides and hilltops. Fortunately much has been done to eliminate the scars, and the Valleys have become much more beautiful over the past fifty years. There are still some coal-mines left but these are kept well and fit into their environment, bringing back only memories of their former industrial glory.

The towns are still strips of terraced houses and I remember the piles of coal that used to be delivered outside each door for the use of the miners' families. Dirty smoke would curl from rows of chimney stacks over the houses, leaving green smog sitting over each town. All that has changed, fortunately, and the towns have been cleaned up.

The town of Ebbw Vale, at the head of a valley, was the home of a huge integrated steelworks when I was a boy, and I worked there as an apprentice when it was in full operation. On one of our visits, I was amazed to find that the blast furnaces and coke ovens had been bulldozed and replaced with "The Garden Festival of Wales". It is an unbelievable transformation and I found it difficult to remember how it was before, but I vividly recall the smells of the coke ovens and the Open Hearth and Bessemer Converter steel furnaces. The Welsh Valleys are definitely worth a visit, especially if you know a little of the history of the area, or have read *How Green is My Valley,* by Dylan Thomas.

Eastern Monmouthshire is mostly rolling green hills with patchworks of cultivated fields. My father farmed some of these fields in the 1920s and 30s in the town of Llanfair Discoed, near the Roman Fortress of Caerwent. Did you know that St. Patrick was born there? Few Irish will acknowledge that St. Patrick was Welsh-- or was he English?

There are many Roman remains in the area, and my father told me of a tumulus in one field, which would yield coins and pottery as he ploughed around it. He had to move a gatepost in one field, as the hole he was digging for it hit a Roman pavement. The pavement is still buried there somewhere.

The Cwm, near Llanfair, has been a favourite spot for me all my life. *Cwm* simply means "valley" in Welsh, but this valley is very special with its rare orchids, carpets of garlic flowers, complex hedgerows, watercress stream and fields of daffodils, bluebells and cowslips in spring. Walking trails take one on circular tours of the whole area from Llanfair Discoed. You can hike up Grey Hill and Mynydd-Alltir-fach (Money Turvey, the locals called it), two old volcanic hills between which is a man-made reservoir. In the same area, the Forester's Oaks, is where the Forest Courts were held. Local dignitaries acted as jurors for these courts for many generations. An old oak tree stood at the road junction and it was here that the sheep stealers were hanged.

In Llanfair Discoed (Saint Mary's Under the Wood), there is a tiny church and on a stone in the porch is the inscription:

"Who Ever hear on Sonday
Will Practis Playing at Ball
it May Be beFore Monday
The Devil Will Have you All."

The Court Farm or Manor House and Llanfair Farm, now known as Lower House, are the principal old buildings of the village and date back to 1635. The old cider house and barn belonging to Llanfair Farm, my father's former property, are now houses. A picturesque pigeon house can be seen alongside the road in the village centre.

The Wye Valley is the border between Monmouthshire and Gloucestershire. From the source to the mouth of the river at Chepstow, where the Wye enters the River Severn, the scenery is superb. Starting at Chepstow, you can visit the old gate to the town, through which all traffic to Wales once had to pass, and the majestic ruined castle at the Wye River bridge. Driving north, you pass the race-course and wind through woodlands, which are carpeted with bluebells in spring, and where the trees turn an unimaginable gold in the Autumn, until you reach the ruins of Tintern Abbey. They have become a little touristy, but it is still worth visiting the Abbey and town. The road criss-crosses the river, which winds its way in horseshoes.

There are numerous small roads worth exploring in the whole valley area and they take you to pretty villages and hamlets with ancient churches and cottages. There are also designated and sign-posted public footpaths connecting each village, pub and church.

At the top of the main valley is the county town of Monmouth. It is home to a prominent boys' school and boasts a statue of Rolls, of Rolls-Royce fame. Monmouth Castle was the birthplace of King Henry the Fifth of England, and his statue is outside the town hall. Ross-on-Wye is noted for its antique shops and its picturesque setting on a hill overlooking the river.

The River Usk is also a river of note and it too meanders in horseshoes through the county. It tends to be a muddy brown at its mouth in Newport, except at high tide, but further upstream it is clear and its deep waters are home to trout and salmon, attracting fishermen from all over the county, country and abroad.

The towns of Usk and Raglan are quiet and historically interesting, and the larger town of Abergavenny, near the Breconshire border, is a bustling market town with many hiking trails to the Skirrid and Sugar Loaf Mountains nearby. Abergavenny is also famous as it was once home for Richard Burton and Elizabeth Taylor.

If you are spending time in Wales, you should explore the Black Mountains and the Brecon Beacons, which are fertile and barren, respectively, giving you contrasts just a few miles apart. This is something that strikes all who visit the Principality of Wales--the great variations in so small a country. West Wales has lovely seaside towns; North Wales has high mountains including Snowdon and Cader Idris.

Dolgellau is a good town from which to explore a little of the coast and the mountains. I nearly bought a hotel there once after visiting it with my friend Michael Hart from Vancouver. The Golden Lion Royal Hotel was situated right in the middle of the town and had been given its Royal designation when several Kings of England stayed there in its early days. I had stayed there myself with my grandparents years ago and still remember the fabulous dinners and wine we enjoyed.

When Michael and I saw it, it had been abandoned for ten years and was in need of significant investment. We saw a challenge and opportunity to get it up and running again, and we could also employ some of our friends and relatives to operate it. The proposal we made was not acceptable, however, and the building was subsequently converted into condominium housing. I am sure that our idea was better and would have done much to bring life back into the hotel and town, which is at the centre of such great touring country.

A tour of North Wales would not be complete without a visit to some of the great castles such as Harlech and Caernarfon, where the Prince of Wales was crowned. Don't underestimate Wales--it is very complex and has much to offer the tourist. Sometimes it is a little difficult to communicate with the locals, especially when they insist on speaking Welsh.

On one occasion, Noreen and I entered a cafe in mid-Wales and immediately everyone stopped talking in English and, after a pause while they stared at us, began to talk in Welsh. They were obviously talking about us foreigners but we had the last laugh, when, as we left, I wished them "Good afternoon" in Welsh.

England

Not far from North Wales are the towns of Chester and Liverpool. They are not remotely similar but should be seen. Chester is noted for its half-timbered Tudor buildings in the centre of the city. Liverpool is the port from which the old sailing ships would leave to collect goods from the British Colonies, and from which many people sailed for the New World. The old dock area has been converted from huge warehouses to new shops, up-market restaurants and tourist attractions. An enormous flea market, where one can buy absolutely anything, operates from one of the unrefurbished buildings on Sundays.

Heading further north, you reach the Lake District, which is Wordsworth's Country and fabulous for walking holidays. It gets very crowded at weekends and in the summer, but we went mid-week in May and found it tranquil and beautiful. There is a large choice of accommodations from pubs to bed and breakfast cottages as well as both small and large hotels to suit every budget.

The situation is the same in the Yorkshire Dales a dozen miles to the east. There are miles of excellent walking country, serviced by pubs at strategic points throughout the Dales, and charming B and B's in quaint little stone cottages set in pretty, old villages. If you choose your time, you can walk for hours and see no people, just sheep, cows, horses and the wild animals of the countryside. There are lots of well-marked footpaths and maps are available from the National Parks offices in several towns in the area.

Scotland

While we are in the north-west of England, it seems logical to continue north across the border of Scotland to

Gretna Green, which was the place to which young English lovers eloped and got married. The Scottish laws were rather more liberal and allowed young marriages, with no waiting for banns to be read over several weeks as in England. Favourite places of mine west of Gretna are Newton Stewart and Glen Troon, scene of a major battle between Scotland and England.

The city of Glasgow has changed for the better over the last couple of decades. It has been cleaned up and the old Victorian buildings are again white after decades of being coated with black grime from the heavy industries which sprang up during the Industrial Revolution. It is now a vibrant city of parks, shops and entertainment.

East of Glasgow, places of note are Peebles, south of Edinburgh, and Edinburgh itself, which, like its poor relation Glasgow, is a must-see. There has always been a friendly rivalry between the neighbouring cities and they speak with totally different accents. Edinburgh has the more cultured accent that is more easily understood by foreigners like myself. North-west of Glasgow is the famous beauty spot of Loch Lomond, which must not be missed. As one continues north, the country becomes more sparsely populated and even more wild and magnificent.

Off the west coast of Scotland lies the Isle of Skye, known through the song of Bonnie Prince Charlie. We were there when the only access was by ferry and it had a real island feeling of isolation. The bridge was under construction and, to me, it is not a real island anymore. It is none the less, a beautiful, tranquil and, in part, barren place. There is nowhere in Scotland that I would not like to visit again.

England

Back in England, I have skipped the north-east as it tends to be more industrial and the weather is cold from the winds whipping across the North Sea. York and the Yorkshire Moors are worth visiting, and I shall always remember days enjoying walks over the heather-clad moors with my daughter, Pippa.

Working your way down the coast, you eventually reach East Anglia, which is an area unique to England. The land is very flat and the winds from the North Sea are ever present; nevertheless, it has attractive countryside and extensive sandy shores. The principal attraction is the Norfolk Broads, which are a network of navigable waterways through the wetlands. This is home for the thousands of temporary and permanently resident waterfowl of many species. It is truly a birdwatcher's paradise.

The city of Norfolk is a great place for browsing in numerous antique shops. One should also visit its magnificent cathedral, whose spire dominates the city and can be seen from many miles away.

From Norfolk, there are straight Roman roads across the plain to Cambridge and on to London. The university town of Cambridge is a town of spires, church bells and, of course, the colleges. You can walk freely around the manicured grounds of many of the colleges where famous scholars have walked for centuries past. Other colleges charge admission or restrict access during term time. One way of getting around easily is by bicycle, as most of the students do. Another way is to rent a boat and punt yourself along the calm canals to get a good look at the "backs" of the colleges.

London could be a chapter or a book of its own. I shall merely list some of my favourite places. The City of London is one square mile at the centre of the great metropolis and can best be seen on foot. Check out St. Paul's Cathedral and the Inns of Court. There are organizations offering walking tours of the City and areas such as Southwark on the South Bank of the Thames, where the old Clink Prison and the reconstructed Globe Theatre are located. Other walks follow the paths of Charles Dickens or take you on pub-crawls of London.

We always visit Harrods department store and ogle at all the fine foods, crystal, furniture and clothes but rarely buy any of their expensive goods. You must walk around Buckingham Palace and watch the colourful changing of the guard there or at the mews near Clarence House. Better still' check out the Horse Guards in Whitehall on your way to see 10 Downing Street, the Houses of Parliament and Westminster Abbey.

A first-time visitor to London can get a great introduction by taking a double decker bus tour. I could go on and on, but if you are visiting England, be sure to spread your time between London and the rest of the country to get a total feel for the country and its people.

Driving due west from London for seventy miles or so, you reach Oxford and the Cotswolds. Oxford is very much like Cambridge and the rivalry between the universities is legendary, both academically and in sports. The Cotswolds is an area of rolling country dotted with villages of beautiful, golden brown Cotswold stone. Villages not to miss are Upper and Lower Slaughter, Broadway, Burford, East Leach, Fairford and Lechlade.

The West of England is perhaps my favourite and one area we never miss on our frequent visits. My ancestors on the Hockey side come from Somerset and Devonshire where they were farmers and butchers. My parents always took family holidays in Devon and Cornwall, and I came to know and love the counties well. Noreen and I always visit Truro in Cornwall and make day trips to places like Mevagissey, St. Ives, Veryan, Portloe and St. Mawes.

We always visit in spring or autumn, as the roads and towns become very crowded in summer and it gets pretty cold in winter. Cornish cream teas are famous and fattening but fabulous. Thick clotted cream is served on freshly baked scones and topped with rich strawberry jam. They are sure to spoil your dinner but they are worth it.

A word about the food in England: it is not always as bad as its reputation. Sure, much of it is still overcooked and stodgy, but you can find true gourmet restaurants serving speciality dishes, such as game, with some of the best wines in the world. The pubs are generally the best for reasonably priced bar food, and it can be washed down with a fresh pint of British beer, served not really cold, but at cellar temperature. Or you might want to try some real Scrumpy--Cider from Devon or Somerset--absolute "heaven."

I apologize to the parts of Britain I have not mentioned, but this dissertation is meant to answer the question I am most frequently asked: "Where shall I go when I visit the United Kingdom?"

Ireland

The way to Ireland is through Wales. I never had a wish to visit the Emerald Isle when I lived in Wales, partly, I believe, because I thought that Wales was so much better--at least on the rugby field. Again, there was strong rivalry between the countries even though the people are mostly Celts. It was only after I married Noreen, whose maiden name is "Connor", that I was persuaded to actually visit Ireland. I am most grateful to her for dragging me there, as we experienced a wonderful three weeks touring the south and west coasts, returning to Wales via Dublin.

To reach Ireland, we took the car ferry from Fishguard, Pembrokeshire (also known as "Little England beyond Wales"), to Rosslare in the south-east corner in the county of Wexford. We actually left our English rent-a-car in Wales and picked up an Irish car in Rosslare. It was at the time when there was still a lot of animosity between the English and the Irish, so the car rental companies didn't want to have English licence plates on their cars in Ireland.

We did not visit the Waterford Crystal factory, which is not far from the ferry as we had visited similar crystal centres near Stourbridge, Worcestershire, England, and were familiar with the process. Perhaps I was a little prejudiced, as I had met Mr. Stewart of Stewart Crystal when I worked in a pub near in Hagley, near Birmingham, years ago. He had given me some of his fine crystal to take to Canada with me, and I have collected it ever since. If you missed seeing Stourbridge or Brierley Hill crystal, then you should probably visit Waterford.

We meandered along the coast, stopping in small towns to get a feel for the country, and stayed in Tramore and Kinsale in Bed and Breakfast accommodation. The Irish Tourist Board lists all approved B & B's and we made our selection by driving past the listed houses and looking at the gardens.

Our experience was that a pretty garden indicated that the owners took a pride in their house too. In every B & B, we enjoyed the huge helpings of Irish bacon, eggs, sausages, tomatoes and mushrooms every morning. In each town we stopped, we checked out the local pubs and their brews. There is nothing like a Guinness, Murphy's, Beamish or Smithwicks drunk in Ireland.

County Cork is where Noreen's mother's family came from, so we naturally had to check out the city of Cork from our B & B in Kinsale. We walked around the city and visited the Protestant Cathedral, and then Noreen rang the bells in the church of St. Ann, Shandon. Blarney Castle is just outside Cork and Noreen had to kiss the famous Blarney Stone. I felt that I had no need to develop my speaking skills.

Driving on along the back roads, we noticed how clean, tidy and well groomed the gardens and fields were. We also noticed that most of the signs were in Gaelic. Friendly locals would wave at our car as we passed - even when they were in cars driving towards us. Sneem was our next stop at the start of The Ring of Kerry. The weather was perfect for a drive around The Ring and we stopped frequently to appreciate the wonderful views over the sea.

We drove through the Gap of Dunloe to Killarney. The Gap of Dunloe is a narrow valley, and open horse carts usually drive visitors over the poor road. We ventured through in our rental car and were glad we did as the heavens opened, soaking all the tourists in their carts. We were disappointed with Killarney, as it was overrun by tourists and scores of huge buses so we drove on to Dingle.

The Dingle Peninsula is beautiful and known for the Dingle Dolphins off the coast. We happened upon a combination cobbler's shop and pub, quite typical of small Irish towns, and found it bustling with activity. It was called "Dick Macs" and we were quickly engaged in conversation with some of the locals. They explained that they were gathering to pay their last respects to a man who had recently died in Italy. He was returning home to be buried in his native Ireland.

The church was opposite the pub, and at exactly eight o'clock, the pub emptied as all the customers left their half-drunk glasses on the bar and tables, and hurried over to the church to view the body. After a short time, they returned to the pub to continue their drinking. There was to be a big funeral the following day and they had to be well prepared.

The following day we drove north through Connor Pass, no doubt named by my wife's ancestors, on through Tralee, and over the River Shannon to Kilkee. The Cliffs of Moher, meaning "Cliffs of ruin" were our next stop, and they were wild and spectacular. The wind whistled over the vertical cliffs and we watched the seabirds catch the drafts and soar overhead. In contrast, our next stop was at the mystical four-thousand-year-old stone slabs called a Dolmen at Ballyvaughan. This is thought to be a burial place for a local chief.

Galway is the town where you catch a ferry to the Aran Islands. We braved a rough sea and sailed to

202 Every Day's a Weekend

Inishmore and walked for miles past tiny fields surrounded by high rock walls. I can only think that they had a lot of rocks to clear before they could grow anything. We heard that the beautiful Aran wool sweaters are now mostly made on the mainland. The scruffy sheep on the island didn't look as if they could produce any wool at all. County Galway boasts Connemara National Park, and we explored this beautiful area from Clifden, a pleasant country town, and the unofficial capital of Connemara. Hikes in the hills near the town offer splendid views towards the Twelve Bens, a row of peaks in a five-mile diameter circle. North of Clifden, in the area of Bangor, we passed through huge bog areas where they still cut the peat to burn in their fireplaces. We continued on to Sligo for a night, before heading towards Dublin through a small part of Northern Ireland.

It was quite scary crossing the border, at that time, as there was considerable tension due to recent car bombings in the centre of Enniskillen. The road was barricaded with barbed wire, and concrete posts could be raised in the road to block traffic completely. There were sand-bagged guard towers manned by camouflaged young British soldiers who were justifiably frightened as they stopped every car crossing the border.

We cleared the border and were merrily driving down the much better roads of Northern Ireland, when a group of men dressed in army fatigues with blackened faces jumped out in front of the car, causing us to brake sharply and stop. We didn't know if they were IRA or British but it turned out they were British soldiers doing a spot check. In the town of Enniskillen, traffic was prohibited from parking on all streets unless a person was sitting in the vehicle. We parked in a designated, secure area and walked around the centre of town. We felt a little uncomfortable with all the security around us, so left to continue our journey to Dublin.

Dublin is a fine city, quite Victorian in architecture, and cut in two by the River Liffey. Moored in the river was a Guinness tanker ship ready to take a load of the black fluid to feed the Irish in England. I had to find the monument to Molly Malone and her barrow and did so in the shopping area of Grafton Street and Henry Street. A highlight of our visit was Sunday morning in Slatteries Pub where hundreds gather for a traditional singsong accompanied by fiddles and spoons. Other places we remember in Dublin include Trinity College, where we saw the Book of Kells, and Phoenix Park, which is nine miles around.

We stayed in bed and breakfast accommodations everywhere in Ireland, and people were all very friendly as long as we identified ourselves as Canadian or Welsh. Next time we shall return as Servas travellers and dig even deeper into the Irish culture and way of life.

Wales

The ferry back to Wales leaves from just south of Dublin and takes you to the Island of Anglesey, which is connected by bridges to the mainland. Our only stop on Anglesey was at the town of

Llanfairpwllgwyngyllgogerychwyndrobwllllantysiliogogogoch,

which boasts the longest place name in Wales. It means Saint Mary's Church in the hollow of the white hazel under a rapid whirlpool and the Church of Saint Tysilio of the red cave. It also happens to be the longest URL (Universal Resource Locator) on the World Wide Web.

Twelve Apostles, Great Ocean Road, Australia

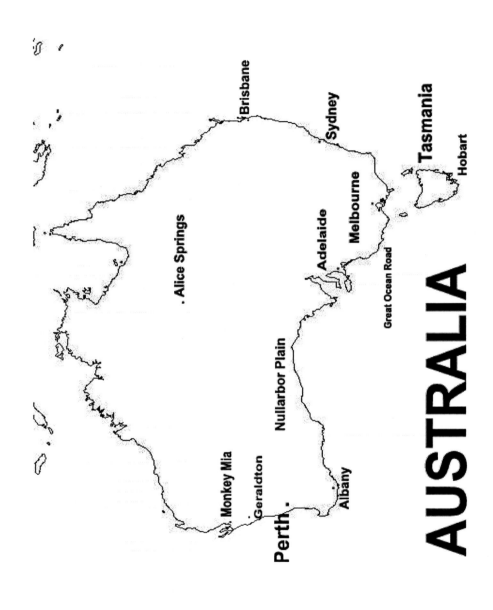

AUSTRALIA

Auckland

North Island

* Rotorua
Lake Taupo
*

Nelson

Arthur's
Pass
*

Wellington
*

Milford
Sound

Mount Cook
*

* Christchurch

South Island

Invercargill
*

* Dunedin

NEW ZEALAND

Chapter 11

Down Under

Australia

Perth, Western Australia, is only a few hours south of Bali, Indonesia, so we have taken the opportunity to visit Perth from Bali on two occasions. Our first visit was towards the end of our first Asian backpacking trip, and the second at the end of a trip to Bali with Hot Tours. In the chapter on Asia, I mentioned that Noreen spent some time in hospital with a virus of some sort, so I was on my own for several days.

Between visits to the hospital, I was able to explore the Perth and Fremantle areas from my base in the hall of residence at the University of Western Australia. If you are ever in a university town when the university is not in session, check out the residences for excellent and inexpensive accommodation. I had a great room with air-conditioning, refrigerator and toaster in a new building set in a beautiful park. It cost less than a room at a downtown hostel.

Perth is a modern city with wide streets and high buildings, and it is remarkably clean and tidy. It was January, and summer there at the time, so it was very hot and the surrounding countryside was brown and dry. The parks in Perth were kept green with irrigation, or reticulation as they call it there. The private gardens were bright with colours and the citizens seemed to take a pride in their city. The downtown shopping precincts were bustling with activity and the shops were filled with merchandise from around the world.

We finished off our stay in Perth visiting friends whom Noreen had met during her travels in eastern Europe some years earlier. It is great to meet up with old friends while travelling, as I have mentioned before, and they showed us all around their beautiful city and also the port of Fremantle next door.

Fremantle had undergone a transformation a year or two before in readiness for the America Cup Yacht Challenge, and was looking very smart. We looked up a couple living in Perth whom we had met on Gili Meno, off Lombok, and they took us out on their yacht in the rough sea off Fremantle. The Australia Day fireworks display over the Swan River in downtown Perth was another highlight. I remember a dozen helicopters circling the crowds on the riverbank and fireworks cascading down the newest and tallest high-rise building.

Sightseeing around Perth is best done by car, as distances can be long, hot and tiring by bus. We did go by bus to Fremantle and take a boat to Rottnest Island, where we cycled for a day, but most of the time we were either driven around by our friends or rented a car. We took one major trip to the south-west corner of Australia, where we saw the old whaling town of Albany. We walked on the cliffs, admired the view and watched some scary blowholes spout water high into the air with a loud boom. We were even more scared when, as it was getting dark, a large animal suddenly jumped in front of us. It was our first kangaroo sighting.

Continuing along the coast, the next day, we saw Peaceful Bay, Williams Bay and the Elephant Rocks and spent hours walking along the gorgeous, deserted beaches. We returned to Fremantle through the Margaret River wine country where tastings are frequent and free. In Fremantle, we encountered a wine festival with more tastings. It was all too much. We enjoyed our three weeks in and around Perth and resolved to return.

The opportunity to return came when we were in Bali again with our Hot Tours group. After three weeks with the group, we sent them back to Vancouver and flew south to Perth. Again we stayed with our friends in South Perth and enjoyed their hospitality, their family, friends and swimming pool. We planned to travel with Servas, the travellers' group we had joined before our trip. We had the host list for Australia and New Zealand and started to telephone hosts in different areas we wanted to explore.

The first host was a day's drive north of Perth at Geraldton on the way to Monkey Mia, a dolphin marine park. We didn't know quite what to expect of our first Servas host home but when we arrived, we were welcomed with a cup of tea and cakes, and immediately relaxed as we chatted to our hostess. We were preparing to ask her for a recommendation for a restaurant when she asked us if we ate chicken; she assumed we would be having dinner at home with them. This was a delightful surprise for us and only then did we realize that Servas hosts almost always provide dinner. This is the time when we exchange information and get to know more about each other and our respective countries.

We talked for a long time and our hosts advised us that the drive to Monkey Mia was a long, hot one and that we should stay there a night and return to our hosts for another night. This was good advice and we resolved to return but to take our hosts out for dinner that night.

Monkey Mia was, indeed, a long, hot drive in 40C(104F) degree heat, but it was dry and not too uncomfortable. We were driving an old Datsun car belonging to a former nursing colleague of Noreen's and we had to limit our speed according to the temperature of the engine. The beach was long, wide and a gorgeous golden colour, and the park was well set-up to handle the tourists and the dolphins who came in to be fed every day--well, almost every day. There are about five days of the year when they don't turn up for some reason and we had chosen two of those five days to be there. We were naturally disappointed, especially as my daughter, Pippa, had been there a year earlier and had raved about the place, telling us to be sure not to miss it.

On our return to Geraldton we stopped to eat a picnic lunch off the road but had to retreat to the car rapidly as we were besieged by millions of blackflies-- one of the hazards of life in the Australian Outback. Another thing I remember about that trip was the "road trains"--immensely long semi-trailer trucks with several trailers that took simply ages to pass. Fortunately the roads are very long and straight, and passing is possible and usually safe.

Back in Geraldton, our Servas hosts had a change of plan and wouldn't let us take them out for dinner, as they had bought some fabulous Australian steaks for us. All we could do was to make a salad and provide some good Australian wine. Such was the overwhelming hospitality of our first Servas host and one that would be repeated many times over by other hosts in Australia and New Zealand.

We returned to Albany where, I had recently discovered, I had six long-lost second cousins. The whole clan came out to visit with us and I enjoyed meeting relatives I hadn't known existed until a year earlier. On the way there and back from Perth we stayed with several Servas hosts. We gained a real feeling and appreciation of the people in Western Australia who are so different and live so remote from the rest of the country. It was Christmas-time, and we spent the holiday time going to parties and concerts with our friends in Perth. Most of the time, people were dressed casually in shorts, which was a little different from our friends in Vancouver.

On Boxing Day, we boarded a bus to Adelaide in South Australia. We thought that there would be lots of space on the bus for the thirty-hour journey but we were wrong. The huge double-decker bus was full for most of the trip, with people getting on and off at every stop. The ride was quite comfortable but the view was pretty boring as we crossed the Nullarbour Plain, a long flat desert with no trees, just low brush.

Half way across the plain, we received a telephone message from the Servas hosts that we were to stay with in Adelaide, but when we telephoned them back, there was no reply. We assumed that they had a problem and couldn't put us up after all, so we would have to stay in a hotel instead.

When we arrived at the bus depot in Adelaide at nine o'clock in the evening, a taxi driver who was sent by our Servas hosts to take us to their home met us. The phone in the taxi rang and it was our hostess, Helen, who explained that her husband was in hospital and she was at work and wouldn't be home until after eleven o'clock. Helen told us where to find the hidden key and which room was ours' and to make ourselves at home.

When she arrived from the hospital where she worked, Helen found us with our feet up in front of the television. Our hostess was not at all concerned with having strangers in her home, as we were Servas travellers. The following day we wanted to rent a car to see the wine country but Helen would have none of that. Her husband, Charlie, was in the hospital and couldn't use his car so we could take his.

The first thing we did was to visit Charlie in the hospital, and we had a great visit with him before starting our tour. By invitation, we stayed an extra night over the normal two nights, then rented a car to continue our drive across Australia.

The drive east from Adelaide took us to Warrnambool near the start of The Great Ocean Road. Our Servas hostess, Andrea, was warm and charming and we became involved with her life by reading stories to her children and checking out her new boyfriend over numerous bottles of wine. It was a hilarious evening. The section along the Great Ocean Road was true to its name and we paused frequently to snap photos, which turned out to be fantastic. The road ended in Melbourne where we stayed with a friend I knew from University in Nottingham some thirty years earlier.

Clare and her husband, Richard, showed us the city, and we also visited even more vineyards in the state of Victoria. Richard had a Rolls Royce motor car and he used his "Roller" to pick up case after case of wine. We were getting to like Australian wines especially their white wines.

Tasmania

Our next destination was the island of Tasmania, because several travellers we had met in Indonesia had insisted we visit them. It was not in our original plan to fly there, but we are most pleased that we did. Tasmania is rather different from the rest of Australia and turned out to be a composite of Australia and New Zealand. It is a large island but is quite laid back, as many small islands are.

We drove first along the north coast and saw beautiful roadside gardens and fields of blue poppies. Much of the world's supply of morphine and heroin comes from Tasmania. We stayed on a farm in Melrose, and from there we took a long hike to Cradle Mountain, which is quite spectacular as it rises steeply from the flat bushland. After seeing our friends in the small town of Launceston, we went to Longford where our Servas hosts treated us to a memorable evening of wine and cheese tastings. They also took us on a lovely bush walk to some waterfalls surrounded by giant tree ferns.

Tasmania is known for its lavender fields, and we were fortunate to be there when the fields were in full bloom, just before they were harvested. We visited the fields and the production facilities on our way to Lala and the home of another Servas host. This host was almost self-sufficient with food from an extensive organic garden. They even owned an organic vineyard. In a large natural pond they had a family of duck-billed platypuses which, obligingly, came out at dusk for us to film them. Previously we had only seen these strange prehistoric animals in a darkened zoo cage.

The next stop was in Orford with a lady who had been a Servas host for many years. She suggested we visit Maria Island National Park, which is on an island nearby. It was once a penal colony, but it is now a nature reserve and we saw many wild wallabies on the island. Another attraction is the "Painted Cliffs," an exquisite, coloured escarpment, carved by the sea.

Our last stop on Tasmania was in the capital, Hobart. We used it as a centre from which to explore the south part of the island. Port Arthur was also a penal colony and has been preserved to show the living conditions of the early convict settlers in Australia. Many Australians go to check their ancestry at the genealogy centre there. I didn't find any Hockeys but my wife found lots of Connors. We took several hikes in the hills around Hobart in Mount Field National Park and Hartz Mountain National Park where we enjoyed the expansive views and the native flora.

It was time to leave Tasmania for New Zealand, but we were delayed by really bad weather that grounded all flights for hours. Severe thunderstorms damaged aircraft and our flight was rerouted through Melbourne and Sydney. The landing in Sydney was one of the most violent we have experienced, so we were pleased to disembark and spend the night in a smart hotel at the airline's expense.

The South Island of New Zealand

We reached Christchurch, New Zealand, the following morning and spent the day wandering around the city. There is a well-marked tourist walk, which makes it easy to catch all the sights and read about them from a guidebook. We took a great excursion from Christchurch to Arthur's Pass National Park where we hiked up into the mountains to enjoy the glorious views and tumbling mountain streams.

After two days in the city, we moved to a lovely home in Governor's Bay where we gazed at a great view from the house over mountains and sea. Before we left the Christchurch area, we attended a potluck lunch for local Servas hosts. The hosts get few travellers wanting to stay so we were asked by several to stay with them when we returned to Christchurch. In fact, they were competing for our custom. Some New Zealanders feel a little isolated and want the world to come to them in the form of seasoned travellers who can tell them stories about other countries.

We pressed on down the east coast through Timaru to the Scottish town of Dunedin, which is built on steep hills that give it great character. Dunedin is actually the ancient Celtic name of Edinburgh. We walked around the University and downtown areas and were given a driving tour by our hosts. I was having some toothache at this point and our hosts were able to refer me to a dentist for antibiotics.

Our next stop was at the bottom of New Zealand, on a farm beyond Invercargill. Only a Servas traveller would find such a remote area and have friends with whom they could stay. It was a thousand-acre sheep farm, and we were immediately pressed into service, rounding up a thousand sheep and moving them into another field. Fortunately we had the help of five wonderful sheepdogs. The farm also boasted a team of Clydesdale horses and the farmer hitched the six magnificent beasts to a plough for us while I took a video of the whole process. He actually uses the horses for ploughing and also shows them in county shows and fairs.

Southland is the name given to the southernmost part of the South Island of New Zealand and we had reached the bottom in Invercargill. Now it was time to head to Fiordland National Park, one of the world's largest National Parks which is in a remote and not fully explored area. The best known part of the park is Milford Sound and a breathtaking road reaches this from Te Anau. The sound itself is explored by boats, which take visitors down the fjord to the open Tasman Sea. Boats pass the soaring tower of Mitre Peak and under waterfalls that cascade vertically down onto the boats. The scenery reminded me of Norway and British Columbia, Canada.

We had planned to stay in Alexandra, Otago, next, but our Servas host there suggested we stay, instead, in her home in Saint Bathans. This is an old gold rush town, badly scarred from mining operations and now almost a ghost town. It is well off the beaten track and we felt fortunate to find it. We would have to use a pretty detailed map to find it again.

After two days walking and relaxing in the hills around Saint Bathans, we continued north and west towards the coast. Our host recommended a route normally used by sheep. We headed off a very small road onto a farmer's property and along a narrow track that wound its way over the hillsides. I was driving and Noreen had to get out of the car seventeen times to open and close gates for me as we worked our way across country.

We saw a wild cat and thousands of sheep but only one person. He was a retired fireman who was panning for gold in a lovely, lonely river that emerged from a deep canyon alongside the track we had followed. The man had retired early with the proceeds of his panning but still returned to pan for pleasure--he showed us some of the golden pleasure in his pan.

Working our way north up the coast, we enjoyed seeing scores of glaciers creeping down from high alpine peaks, through temperate rainforests to the ocean. The highest peak is snow-covered Mount Cook, which we had seen from the east as we left Christchurch. At the north end of the South Island of New Zealand is Nelson, where we stayed for four days. Our hosts took us all around the area and showed us a Kiwifruit orchard, and the hill, which is the geographic centre of New Zealand. We stayed at a beautiful estate called "Gardens of the World", which had been created by a retired nurseryman.

Nelson is a good place from which to explore the Abel Tasman National Park, known for its golden beaches. East of Nelson is the Marlborough Sounds Maritime Park, an extensive inland waterway system that flows between beautiful forest-clad hillsides. Hiking is a popular hobby for New Zealanders, but they will understand you better if you refer to it as tramping or bush walking. Nelson itself is a lively centre of commerce and I am sure there are lots of things to keep people busy, whatever their interests. I would consider living there myself if it wasn't so far from the rest of the world.

We had hoped to visit Blenheim, which is famous for its annual wine festival, but we happened to arrive when the festival was under way, so accommodation was impossible to find. Even the local Servas hosts had friends camped out on their lawns. We had reached the north end of the South Island of New Zealand and had been impressed by the whole island. We were impressed by the fantastic unspoiled scenery and by the very warm welcome we had received from the people. Other Canadians we had met shared this impression. One couple, who were travelling by bicycle and flying a Canadian flag, had been stopped numerous times and been invited to peoples' homes for meals and overnight accommodation. Hospitality has been raised to the highest level in New Zealand.

New Zealand's North Island

The ferry ride from Picton on the South Island to Wellington on the North Island takes you through the Marlborough Sounds and is a most picturesque boat trip. We were welcomed into Wellington harbour by literally hundreds of boats. It was the day that a round-the-world race of big sailing boats was starting the leg of the race that would take them to Sydney, Australia. Tall ships, naval ships and all kinds of pleasure craft accompanied the racers through stormy seas while helicopters hovered overhead. We watched the racers carve their way through the rough waters with every square inch of their sails flying and filled. We were fortunate to see them all again in Sydney harbour a few weeks later, this time moored alongside the dock at the conclusion of the race.

Wellington is a busy New Zealand city, but busy by New Zealand standards is quiet compared with North America or Europe. The gardens are beautiful in this capital city, and the setting in the hills looking south over the natural harbour is lovely. First we stayed downtown and visited the government buildings and cosmopolitan shops, then we moved to a farm on the outskirts of the city.

It was an organic hobby farm and it was where we met our first "Woofer." "Willing Workers on Organic Farms" is an organization, similar to Servas, who offer free accommodation in return for assistance in running the farm. Normally the participants are young people who stay for several weeks, but people are not discriminated against because of their age. We too, as Servas travellers, were put to work and enjoyed ourselves while clearing land for a new garden.

The road north of Wellington winds through countryside that reminds me of England and Wales. In fact, we stopped to visit someone we had met at a friend's farm in Wales a year earlier. We love to collect names and addresses of people as we travel and frequently have the opportunity of meeting them in their home town at a later date. They are usually able to direct us to some local place that normal tourists would never find. This time was no exception and we found a trail in a National Park where we tramped with the locals into wild areas of rocks on unstable mountains and alongside rushing mountain streams.

Near Lake Taupo, we stayed with a host who asked us if there was something we had not done in New Zealand that we really wanted to do. One thing that we had not done was to meet a Maori person and talk to them about their heritage. We were immediately taken across the road to a neighbour who was a Maori and a retired schoolteacher. We were entertained with an evening of interesting discussion on the people and culture.

All the following day, the Maori lady took us to see secret Maori places in the forests and on the mountains. We were taken to a village that was off-limits to non-Maoris where we saw ancient rock carvings, hot springs and mud-pools on the edge of Lake Taupo. It was a very spiritual day, and one that we shall always remember.

Lake Taupo and the town of Taupo are pleasant but touristy, and this goes for Rotorua, famous for the hot springs and geothermal generating plants. Do visit these places but be prepared for the crowds. If you have the chance, get off the beaten track, explore the back roads and meet the people. We found a Servas host with a guest ranch, but we stayed in their home. Before dinner, we had to earn our keep by going on horseback to round up a herd of cows. It took us over beautiful green hills with marvellous views over fields of sheep and cattle. We witnessed a great sunset before returning, tired but happy, to a gourmet dinner with fine New Zealand wines. Life can be tough sometimes.

Auckland is a big, cosmopolitan city, almost surrounded by water. Known as the "City of Sails," it is really true to its name. You don't have to like boats to appreciate the scenery. We visited friends who had moved to Auckland from Vancouver and also New Zealanders I had met in Hamilton, Ontario, thirty years ago. Yes, I do keep in touch with people for a long time.

Our friends took us on extensive tours of the city, which is becoming well developed with high-rise office buildings, fancy restaurants and natural parks to complement its nautical setting. It is the jumping-off point for excursions to the Bay of Islands on the northern tip of the North Island. It is an area of natural coastal beauty and islands, and it encompasses several nature reserves. Historically, it is important to New Zealand because a treaty was signed there between the Whites and Maoris in the mid nineteenth century.

In summary, New Zealand is a young country with strong historical connections through the Maori natives and the British settlers. It is a land of outstanding natural beauty, populated by some of the most friendly and hospitable people we have met. The pace of life is slow and relaxed and it could be an ideal retirement haven for those who don't need to travel the world as we do. Travel inside the country is easy but it gets expensive to fly abroad, and it is a long way to Europe and America.

Eastern Australia

Sydney was our final stop in Australasia and we made it our base for a week while we explored the city and areas to the north and south. We stayed with a Servas host in Annandale, close to the centre of Sydney, and were directed to the usual tourist spots and to local restaurants where there were no tourists. We looked up several friends I had met on an earlier trip to Australia and others we had met while travelling in Indonesia.

Sydney is an exciting, vibrant city by day and by night. The Opera House and Sydney Harbour Bridge were "must-sees," of course, as were Bondi and Manly Beaches. We walked the Circular Quay, Darling Harbour, Paddington and Kings Cross, and visited the newest museum, which is dedicated to the Holocaust.

The Convention Centre at Darling Harbour is a huge development and was being readied for the influx of visitors expected for the year 2000 and the Olympic Games. It was here that we were able to meet some of the participants in the round-the-world yacht race. They were just getting over a rough crossing from New Zealand and preparing to continue around the Cape of Good Hope to England.

Many activities in and around Sydney are free; even museums are free on some days. Swimming in the harbour is a local pastime and swimmers are protected from sharks by huge shark nets, but we were still not tempted to swim ourselves, as the water is both cool and somewhat polluted. We could have stayed for a month and still been busy every day visiting new sights, but we wanted a taste of rural Australia too.

North of Sydney we found numerous sandy beaches and eucalyptus forests, and there was lots of opportunity for bush walking. It is interesting that the national fascination for trekking in both Australia and New Zealand has developed distinctly different terms for the sport. It was soon evident to us that distances are so vast in Australia that it would take months to cover it by car. The topography is similar for huge areas, and a better way to see the country would be to fly to specific areas and explore on a local basis. I had explored the east coast in this manner on a previous visit and covered Brisbane, the Gold Coast, Rockingham, Cairns and the Great Barrier Reef in a few weeks.

We returned to Sydney and headed south through some awe-inspiring forests and past long, deserted beaches. No matter which road we took, there were scenic routes everywhere. Servas hosts welcomed us in several small towns, and I even participated in a local tennis tournament one evening.

We finished our time in Australia back in Sydney with our Servas friends and vowed to return sometime. We reflected on the friendly competition between Tasmania and the mainland of Australia and that between the North and South Islands of New Zealand. Of course, there is even greater competition between Australia and New Zealand. It is hard to compare them as they all have unique characteristics, so I shall refrain from showing any favouritism.

We felt quite at home on all four islands and enjoyed ourselves immensely. They are a long way from Vancouver and not sufficiently different to warrant the expense of frequent visits. There are still some two hundred countries in the world we have not yet seen!

Epilogue

This book covers only the first ten years of our retirement. It includes most of the highlights of our travels but many stories are still untold. We intend to carry on travelling for as long as we are able and to collect more anecdotes as we do.

We have already completed an extensive tour of southern Africa that will surely be the topic of a book. The mode of travel was mainly by local bus, but we also travelled on one upscale safari and in rental cars. We have a tendency to treat ourselves a little more gently these days, as we grow a little older. We never lose sight of the fact that the most interesting aspect of life is the people we meet. To this end, we try to mingle with local people in the countries we traverse and local buses and camping safaris helped us to do this in Africa.

Future plans include taking more groups to Bali and now also to Borneo. Independent travel will take us to the Philippines, South America, India and Nepal. Noreen has always wanted to visit Afghanistan too, but the political situation may prevent that for some time.

Europe will be more appealing as we get older and less mobile, as travel there is so easy. It is more expensive than third world travel but maybe our teak trees will bear fruit and provide us with the necessary income. I can see no immediate end to our travelling, but there will inevitably be a slowdown.

I received a reminder of my mortality a couple of years ago, when I fell off my bike in front of a large Mercedes car. It ran right over my chest, breaking five ribs and collapsing one lung. My back suffered road rash and there many cuts and bruises. I wound up in an intensive care ward for a week followed by a further three weeks in hospital. My doctor was pleased with my rapid recovery and put it down to my physical fitness at the time of the accident. We had been doing a lot of cycling in the mountains around Vancouver that summer. We continue to cycle for fitness as much as we can.

Our long-term goal is to sell our townhouse and move to a small cottage with a large garden and a greenhouse. This will allow me to pursue my hobby of gardening and provide space for two Golden Retriever dogs and a Siamese cat. We have yet to establish a location for the dream retirement cottage as funds are limited and desirable locations such as West Vancouver are very expensive. One option we have is to move to Vancouver Island where property is much less expensive, but I have yet to convince Noreen that this is the right area.

Appendix - Chronology

<u>1990</u>
September	Retired.
September - October	England, Wales, Italy.
February	England, Wales.

<u>1992</u>
May - July	England, Wales, Ireland.
October	Hong Kong, China, Macau.
October - December	Thailand, Indonesia.

<u>1993</u>
January - March	Indonesia, Australia, Singapore, Malaysia
May	England
October - December	Costa Rica.

<u>1994</u>
January - April	Costa Rica, Columbia, Ecuador.
September - October	England, Wales, Ireland, Scotland.

<u>1995</u>
September - October	1st Group to Bali & Lombok, Indonesia.

<u>1996</u>
February - April	Honduras, Guatemala.
October	2nd Group to Bali & Lombok.
November	Spice Islands, Bali, Indonesia.
December	Perth, Australia.

<u>1997</u>
January   Cross Australia, Tasmania.
February   New Zealand.
March   Eastern Australia.
December   1st Drive to Central America
<u>1998</u>
January - April   Honduras, Panama, Costa Rica
April   1st Drive from Honduras,
                                 Guatemala, Mexico & U.S.A.

<u>1998</u>
October   3rd Group to Bali & Lombok.
November   Borneo, Japan.
<u>1999</u>
January   2nd Drive to Honduras.
February - March   Hurricane relief, Honduras.
May   England, Wales.
November   4th Group to Bali & Lombok.
December   Peninsular Malaysia.
<u>2000</u>
January - March   Honduras.
April   2nd Drive Back from Honduras.
                                 Guatemala, Belize, Mexico &
                                 U.S.A.

Appendix - List of Maps

Appendix - List of Photographs

Noreen and Newton in Vancouver

Rice terraces, Central Bali, Indonesia

Noreen, Ayu and son in Puri Saraswati, Ubud, Bali

Sunset over Gunung Agung Volcano, Bali, from Lombok

Ancient Village, Lombok, Indonesia

Author with Rafflesia Flower, Sarawak, Borneo

Tunku Abdul Rahman Park near Kota Kinabalu, Sabah,

Author with Jairo at his home near Trujillo, Honduras

Noreen issuing blankets in San Juan Chimula, Chiapas,

Chiapas Indians

Mayan Pyramid at Chichenitza, Yucatan, Mexico

Noreen and Newton on Pat and Joska's Harley in Mexico

Yorkshire Dales, England

Twelve Apostles, Great Ocean Road, Victoria, Australia

Appendix - Useful Resources

Servas International	**www.servas.org**
Servas U.K.	**www.servasbritain.u-net.com**
Home Exchange	**www.homelink.org**
Air Travel	**www.skyauction.com** **www.flyaow.com**
Honduras News	**www.marrder.com/htw**
Hot Tours	**www.itsmyholiday.com/hot_tours** E-mail: **hot_tours@hotmail.com**
Government Canada	**www. voyage.dfait-maeci.gc.ca/destinations /menu_e.htm**
U.S.	**http://travel.state.gov/travel_warnings.html**
Vancouver	**www.visitvancouver.com**
Lonely Planet Guide	**www.lonelyplanet.com**
Best Search Engines	**www.dogpile.com**

ISBN 155212819-9

9 781552 128190